Doing Classroom Research

Doing Classroom Research: A Step-by-step Guide for Student Teachers

Edited by
Sally Elton-Chalcraft, Alice Hansen
and Samantha Twiselton

 Open University Press

Open University Press
McGraw-Hill Education
McGraw-Hill House
Shoppenhangers Road
Maidenhead
Berkshire
England
SL6 2QL

email: enquiries@openup.co.uk
world wide web: www.openup.co.uk

and Two Penn Plaza, New York, NY 10121-2289, USA

First published 2008

A catalogue record of this book is available from the British Library

ISBN-13: 9780335228768 (pb)   9780335228751 (hb)
ISBN-10: 0335228768 (pb)   0335228755 (hb)

Library of Congress Cataloging-in-Publication Data
CIP data applied for

Fictitious names of companies, products, people, characters and/or data that may be used herein (in case studies or in examples) are not intended to represent any real individual, company, product or event

Typeset by BookEns Ltd, Royston, Herts.
Printed in the UK by Bell and Bain Ltd, Glasgow

The **McGraw·Hill** Companies

Contents

Figures and tables

Contributors

Adrian Copping is an experienced primary practitioner. He is currently working as a senior lecturer in English and Literacy at the University of Cumbria, teaching and developing both primary curriculum and specialism courses. As well as working on undergraduate courses, Adrian has been significantly involved in developing a Masters level PGCE at the university, which has included co-authorship of a practitioner research module.

Sandra Eady is an Education Studies tutor teaching mostly on the Postgraduate Primary and the Masters in Education programmes at the University of Cumbria (UoC). She joined UoC after lecturing at Canterbury Christ Church University and prior to that taught for 13 years in a range of primary schools. She is scholarship and research co-ordinator at UoC and her research interests lie within educational policy and practice and currently focus on teachers' professional development in primary and secondary schools.

Sally Elton-Chalcraft taught in a range of junior, infant and middle schools in Oxfordshire and Derbyshire and worked at two other ITE institutions before joining St Martin's College, now the University of Cumbria where she is Course Leader for Religious Studies and Primary QTS. She has an MA and PhD and has researched and published in the areas of children's spirituality and multicultural education.

James Fraser (*BA, MA*) is a Senior Learning Advisor at the University of Cumbria. He has been an advocate of Information Fluency skills within the University for six years and in 2006 was awarded a Teaching Fellowship in recognition of his work done in this area. James has presented at various national conferences on the topic of Information Fluency and is committed to supporting students to become independent and confident users of information.

Sarah Hall has worked as a Religious Studies teacher in secondary education for one year following the completion of a Biblical Studies PhD and PGCE. Her specific interests are Judaism, Holocaust Education and embedding Thinking Skills and PLTs within the secondary curriculum. She lives in Manchester and currently works in Oldham.

Alice Hansen is a Principal Lecturer at the University of Cumbria. Before coming to the university, she taught extensively in England and abroad. She is the Programme Leader for the Full-time Primary Postgraduate Certificate of Education. Her background is in primary mathematics education and information communications technology (ICT) education. Her research interests are varied and involve looking at how children construct definitions of quadrilaterals, the impact of ICT on learning and teaching, PGCE M-level study, and design research methodology.

Des Hewitt is Assistant Head of Teacher Education at the University of Derby. He leads the Primary Initial Teacher Education team and teaches BEd, PGCE, MA and EdD students. While the principal focus of teaching is primary English, Des also teaches research methods at undergraduate and postgraduate level studies. Working with others is an incredibly stimulating experience, whether it be in relation to 'the assessment lives of student teachers', 'diversity in schools' or 'implementation of *Every Child Matters*' through Local Authority Integrated Children's Services teams (all current areas of research). He has recently published several books: Parker-Jenkins, M., Hewitt, D., Brownhill, S. and Sanders, T. (2007) *Aiming Higher: Diversity in Schools*, London: Paul Chapman Publishing and Hewitt, D. (2008) *Understanding Effective Learning*, OUP. Des's research background started as a teacher in school with questions about independent learning. This led finally to a PhD thesis: 'self-support learning strategies in English'.

Hannah Hough (BSc, MSc, PGCLTHE) is the Head of Academic Services at the University of Cumbria, leading the Information Fluency skills agenda across the institution. She also sits on the CILIP Information Literacy Group as Training Officer, co-ordinating national CPD workshops for information professionals. Hannah has a professional interest in embedding key skills into the curriculum, bridging the skills gaps that can emerge between all levels of study.

Dennis Howlett worked in Inner London as a Primary School Teacher before serving as an Advisory Teacher for the same authority. Since that time, and for nearly 20 years he has been practising and developing the art of Creative and Effective teaching in higher education! He has been lecturing in primary science education and is currently developing the Creative and Effective teaching module for the Postgraduate course.

Ruth Jones has worked in primary education for over 13 years, her specific interests are early years' education and maths. Following a year on a secondment teaching problem-solving she is currently working on her dissertation to enable her to be awarded an MA. She has two children and lives in Cumbria with her husband.

Martyn Lawson After a long career in the Armed Forces, Martyn Lawson taught ICT in an independent secondary school in North Yorkshire before moving into higher education. He is currently Co-ordinator for Secondary Initial Teacher Education for the University of Cumbria where he also teaches on ICT Specialist courses.

Patricia Macpherson is Head of the Division of Childhood, Adolescent and Creative Studies at the University of Cumbria. She has a background in teaching and education for children and young people in nursery through to secondary settings. She has a strong interest in and wide experience of identifying and responding to ethical issues in educational settings.

Mike Ollerton After failing the 11+ Mike spent three years in the bottom stream in a technical school in Burnley. In 1968 he was accepted on a primary/secondary teacher training course. He taught for two years in Lowca Primary School and 12 years at Wyndham Comprehensive School, Egremont. Mike was a Head of Mathematics in a Telford school where he led the development of mixed-attainment teaching across the 11–16 age range. In 1989 he gained his first degree through the Open University. He taught at St Martin's College from 1995 until 2005. In 1997 he gained his MPhil, also through the Open University. Mike has written many articles, several chapters and four books. These include Ollerton, M. (2003) *Getting the Buggers to Add Up*, London and New York: Continuum and Ollerton, M. (2005) *100 Ideas for Teaching Mathematics*, London and New York: Continuum. Mike is now a freelance mathematics educator.

Carey Philpott was a secondary school English teacher working mostly in London before he moved into teaching in higher education. He currently works with primary and secondary ITE students at the University of Cumbria. He is also the programme leader for the secondary PGCE programme.

Sue Pope was Head of Science Education at St Martin's College when this chapter was first conceived. Since then she has moved to QCA as programme manager for mathematics. Her background is in mathematics education. After 10 years teaching in schools she worked as a mathematics advisor and then spent 10 years in initial teacher education working at the University of Surrey, Roehampton before St Martin's College, Lancaster.

Deborah Roberts is an experienced primary classroom practitioner. As a former senior lecturer in Initial Teacher Education at the University of Cumbria, she has worked with both undergraduate, PGCE and Masters students, teaching on research-related courses and supervising research projects. She is currently researching and working freelance within the ITE sector.

Helen Scott has worked in art and design education since 1991. She taught in the secondary and post-16 sectors, leading a range of courses. From 2000 to 2005, she ran the PGCE Secondary Art and Design course at St Martin's College in Lancaster. She currently runs the MA in Education at the University of Cumbria and teaches PGCE and under-graduate students of art and design. Her PhD research involves critical studies in secondary art and design education.

Edward Tyson is a Senior Lecturer in the Division of Primary ICT and Education at the University of Cumbria. He has a background in teaching and education in primary and middle school settings. While completing his recent MA in Education he became aware for the need to synchronize ethical issues with research methodology.

Samantha Twiselton is Associate Dean in the Education Faculty of the University of Cumbria. She was a primary teacher for a number of years before joining the Initial Teacher Education sector and gaining her PhD that focused on the developing beliefs, values and understandings of student teachers as progressed through their initial teacher education. She is a primary English specialist and was formerly the primary PGCE Programme Leader at the University of Cumbria. She is a passionate believer in the importance of evidence-based teaching and strongly encourages all her students to see research as central to good practice. She lives in the Lake District with her husband and two children and one day might find the time to take a walk in it.

Foreword

This book marks a milestone in the teaching profession in the sense that it is designed to support, celebrate and value the role of school-based research in being, and learning to become, an effective classroom practitioner. It is the final outcome of a collaborative venture involving a range of tutors and student researchers at the University of Cumbria (formerly St Martin's College), the University of Derby, Lancaster University and the QCA. All those involved have direct experience of and expertise in school-based research and they are all passionate about its importance to the role and identity of the teacher.

As there are moves afoot to develop teaching into a Masters-level profession, it would appear the time is right to promote a model of teaching that sees evidence-based, enquiry-driven practice as central to effective classroom practice. This model is surely of critical importance if education is to have an impact on the lives of individuals, communities and society, for it is through critical reflection that practice improves. The book not only promotes such a model but also provides a practical step-by-step source of support for those who are experiencing it.

Dr Neil Simco
Dean of Education
University of Cumbria

Part I Introduction

1 What's in it for me?

Sally Elton-Chalcraft, Alice Hansen and Samantha Twiselton

Introduction

This book is underpinned by a simple philosophy: *all good teachers desire to improve their practice.* This chapter develops this basic premise and introduces a number of themes within that philosophy that other chapters develop.

The aims of the chapter are to help you:

- appreciate the value of school-based research;
- understand the connection between effective teaching and research.

Why conduct school-based research?

For many student teachers the obvious answer to this question will be 'Because I have to – it's for one of my assignments'. Yet if you can see a value to it that goes beyond this it will help you to carry out your research in a way that has a direct value for your teaching. This should have the double benefit of making you focused and also helping you to avoid feeling resentful about doing something that is 'extra' to your main role in the classroom.

For some people the idea of 'teacher as researcher' may seem a little difficult. We all know how many demanding requirements teachers face already – any additions may feel like the final straw. However, this point of view is only valid if you do not think that teachers need to have an evidence base in order to make the best decisions. If you agree that good teaching is based on thorough and tested knowledge about what does and does not work, the research element becomes a little easier to bear.

In fact, nearly all teachers and student teachers accept that 'what works for these children?' is a question they are constantly asking and trying to answer. Every time you reflect on a lesson (either formally through evaluations or informally as you draw breath when the children leave the room) you are likely to be at least partially grappling with this question. In this sense, all those who ask it are on the road to being researchers. This book shows you ways of making gut reactions into something that has been systematically tried, tested and compared to other people's work. As Stenhouse (1975) claimed, research is 'systematic enquiry made public'. This book is designed to help you do this in a way that will make you into a better teacher.

Reflective practice

The English Professional Standards for Teachers (Training and Development Agency for Schools 2007) reflect and validate our philosophy and this helps in showing how practitioner research will help you to meet the QTS standards, if you are training in England. The Standards are set within a framework of three interrelated sections: professional attributes, professional knowledge and understanding, and professional skills. As a tool to support teachers in identifying their professional development needs, there is an inherent aspect to all three sections that involves reflective practice. Indeed, it is intended that the Standards are used as 'a backdrop to discussions about how a teacher's performance should be viewed in relation to their current career stage and the career stage they are approaching' (TDA 2007: 3) and there are clear expectations that student teachers begin their careers with reflective practice under-pinning their initial teacher education experience within the QTS Standards and that this will then continue throughout their careers.

The term 'reflection' was originated by Dewey around 100 years ago (1915), yet there is still no concise definition. However, we offer Hussein's explanation of how reflection:

> enables practitioners to analyze, discuss, evaluate and change their own practice, adopting an analytical approach towards their practice, and encourages them to appraise the moral and ethical issues implicit in classroom practices, including the critical examination of their own beliefs about good teaching.
>
> (TDA 2007: 190)

Abou Baker El-Dib (2007) explains how introducing reflection in teacher education programmes – a relatively recent evolution – necessitated the need for measuring evaluation. Many models attempt to explain the role of reflection in learning and some relate these directly to teacher education (for example, Van Manen 1977; Schoen 1987; Brookfield 1995; Galvez-Martin *et al*.1998). These suggest that there are various stages of professional competence that are achieved through reflection. For example, Pollard (2008) offers a developmental model of teaching that takes teachers from 'beginning teaching' in which the focus is on routine and 'survival', through to a fourth and final stage 'reflective teaching' in which student teachers are 'taking control and developing professionalism' (www.tlrp.org/rtweb-pa). Models such as these remind us how complex educational settings are. However, we would like to suggest that policy developments like the Professional Standards and a sector move to offering Master level PGCE validates for student teachers, perhaps for the first time, the importance of becoming reflective practitioners from the earliest stages of their careers, beyond 'teacher training' to developing their practice within their 'teacher education'.

From reflective practitioner to teacher researcher

If you have had any placement experience at all you will know that teaching and learning is an incredibly complicated business. There are so many variable factors involved – learning styles, motivation, room layout, self-esteem, cognitive awareness, emotional intelligence and task design to name but a few. One of the most stressful aspects of teaching is trying to find your way through all these to create a successful learning experience. It can feel like you are fumbling around in the dark or that you are blindly following ways of doing things without knowing why.

If you were about to undergo brain surgery and you overheard the surgeon explaining that his approach was something along the lines of 'I'll try it this way – see how it goes – I can always think of something else if it doesn't work', imagine how you would feel! It is reasonable, if not absolutely non-negotiable, that we expect the work of the people in whose hands we put our lives to have a good evidence base under-pinning their actions. If we do not always expect them to have conducted published research themselves, we do at least expect them to have got their information from a tried and tested source and that they also use their own experience to shape and hone it. Teaching is one of *the most* important professions (it shapes the lives of children and society) and no one should expect teachers to act either through random guess work or to follow slavishly instructions from others without knowing the evidence base that informs them. This book aims to provide a step-by-step guide that will support you through your education as practitioner/teacher and researcher.

Magos (2007: 1103) offers an explanation of how action research should have a place within initial teacher education. He refers to 'the active and initial role a teacher should have in his/her training' and to 'the need to bridge the daily educational practice with the broad academic theory and the teaching with the research'. Magos found that changes were twofold in student teachers who undertook research on their placements. These involved both changes to the student teachers' professional role and to their ideological beliefs. Magos's research was concerned with aspects wider than pupils' academic achievement. It is possible, and positively encouraged in this book, to focus your research on aspects that are broader than the National Curriculum or the Primary National Strategy. For example, developing the whole child is a theme in Chapters 5 and 8 where ethical issues, innovative and creative teaching are discussed.

Hussein (2007: 190) highlights how reflection aids student teachers in developing their own sense of responsibility to develop their own ideas about effective teaching. 'It helps them to develop their own theories and empowers them to take a more active role in educational decision making.' These aspects are considered in Chapters 2, 5 and 13, in relation to student teachers becoming more effective by improving their own teaching and their pupils' learning. Additionally, school improvement is an issue that is revisited in many of the chapters in this book (for example, Chapters 7, 8, 9 and 10) and naturally remains high on schools' agendas.

Smith (2007) also explores how student teachers and newly qualified teachers develop their professional identity and knowledge through placement experience. He highlights the complexity of the many temporary contexts that student teachers find themselves in, and cautions us by citing Britzman (2003, cited in Smith 2007) who revealed that 'even though student-teachers have great hopes for experience and see it almost as a cure for ignorance, it comes in various forms and it is not always clear how experience is used, at the time or with hindsight' (Smith 2007: 393).

Sharing your practice with others

We conclude this chapter by considering the need to share our research with others. Hargreaves (2000, cited in Aubusson *et al.* 2007: 135) reminds us that 'there is often limited sharing of what happens in the classroom and professional knowledge remains isolated with individual teachers and relatively unscrutinised'. However, Feiman-Nemser (2001: 1042) reminds us that 'by engaging in professional discourse with like-minded colleagues grounded in the content and tasks or teaching and learning, teachers can deepen their knowledge of subject matter and curriculum, refine their instructional repertoire, hone their inquiry skills and become critical colleagues'. Indeed, Aubusson *et al.* reflect on the notion of a teacher community being a

> community of learners' that is characterized by 'sharing knowledge, progressive discourse involving identification of phenomena of significance and discussion advancing understanding of it; mutual respect; the development of collective expertise surpassing that of individuals; genuine enquiry; and a determination to improve communities in which professional learners engage and which they value.
>
> (2007: 134)

Through sharing our practice with others, ethical issues (as discussed in Chapters 2 and 5 particularly) are embedded within your practice. Additionally, the validity and reliability of the claims you make are scrutinized by your peers (see Chapters 2 and 6). For us, one of the greatest reasons for making your practice public is that it gives you a voice in the world in which you are operating and the potential to influence not only other people's practice but even possibly policy decisions.

In the recent past, some (see, for example, Siskin 1994) suggested that because of the complexity of educational settings it is not possible to develop a community of practice and instead knowledge remains with teachers in their classrooms, not open to scrutiny by others. Indeed, Chapters 2, 5 and 8 consider the complex situation teachers find themselves in and in Chapter 5 there is discussion about cultural positions of acceptance regarding what is good practice. Chapters 6 and 10 remind us how it is important to be wary of making over-generalizations from small-scale research projects.

A culture shift for the teaching profession?

Aubusson *et al.* (2007) raise a question about the extent to which reflective practice is informative or transformative. They suggest that a transformation is required to develop a mature professional learning community and they provide specific but complex examples of where this has happened. We are reminded by others (for example Pomson

2005) that this community of practice will not happen spontaneously. Aubusson *et al.* (2007: 146) suggest that the teaching profession require 'teachers bold enough' to use the available scaffolding, which in England, are areas such as the TDA Professional Standards, many post-graduate level initial teacher education programmes and post-graduate professional development (PPD) (www.tda.gov.uk/partners/cpd/ppd.aspx) to create a 'new level of community interaction'.

To boldly go . . .

We offer you this challenge. Do you want to be a teacher who is able, wittingly, to challenge and develop your own and others' practice by systematic enquiry? Are you able to develop your own teaching in light of your findings? To what extent are you, as a student or novice teacher, able to support your colleagues in developing their own practice or the school improvement plan?

The TDA, through the Professional Standards (which is underpinned by Every Child Matters), encourages us to become more effective teachers. Through practitioner research, will you?

If the answer to this challenge is a resounding 'yes', then this book will help you to do this. The specific skills you may require to undertake your research are reviewed in Chapter 4 (information fluency skills), Chapters 2, 3 and 7 (finding a research focus), Chapter 7 (methodology and method), Chapters 6, 10 and 11 (data analysis) and very importantly Chapters 3 and 7 discuss managing the competing demands on your time.

At the beginning of your initial teacher education and the research elements of your course you may feel like a novice, a beginner or 'emergent' reflective practitioner and researcher. At the end, and after the submission of your research project, we are confident you will emerge as a 'competent newly qualified' practitioner researcher, who appreciates the importance of seeing teaching as a research-based profession. This book aims to support you as you progress from 'emergent' to 'competent' practitioner researcher, committed to perso-nal and school development. There is evidence of student teachers who have engaged in research, reaped the benefits of it, and published (Cain *et al.* 2007). We hope that you will continue to develop as a practitioner researcher and perhaps enrol on an MA or MEd programme to sustain your interest and maintain continued support that you will have experienced during your Initial Teacher Education phase, and dissemi-nate your present and future research. Good luck and welcome to the research-based profession of teaching!

References

Abou Baker El-Dib, M. (2007) Levels of reflection in action research: an overview and an assessment tool, *Teaching and Teacher Education*, 23: 24–35.

Aubusson, P., Steele, F., Dinham, S. and Brady, L. (2007) Action learning in teacher learning community formation: informative or transformative? *Teacher Development*, 11(2): 133–48.

Brookfield, S. (1995) *Becoming a Critically Reflective Teacher*. San Francisco: Jossey-Bass.

Cain, T., Holmes, M., Larrett, A. and Mattock, J. (2007) Literature-informed, one-turn action research: three case studies and a commentary *British Educational Research Journal*, 33(1): 91–106.

Dewey, J. (1915) *Schools of Tomorrow*. London: Dent.

Feiman-Nemser, S. (2001) From preparation to practice: designing a continuum to strengthen and sustain teaching, *Teachers College Record*, 103(6): 1013–55.

Galvez-Martin, M., Bowman, C. and Morrison, M. (1998) An exploratory study of the level of reflection attained by preservice teachers, *Mid-Western Educational Researcher*, 11(2): 9–18.

Hargreaves, D.H. (2000) Cited in P. Aubusson, F. Steele, S. Dinham and L. Brady (2007) Action learning in teacher learning community formation: informative or transformative? *Teacher Development*, 11(2): 133–48.

Hussein, J. W. (2007) Experience gained through engaging student teachers in a developmental reflective process, *Teacher Development*, 11(2): 189–201.

Magos, K. (2007) The contribution of action-research to training teachers in intercultural education: a research in the field of Greek minority education, *Teaching and Teacher Education*, 23: 1102–12.

Pollard, A. (2008) *Reflective Teaching*, www.tlrp.org/rtweb-pa/, accessed 15 February 2008.

Pomson, A. (2005) Parochial school satisfactions: what research in private Jewish day school reveals about satisfactions and dissatisfactions in teachers' work, *Educational Research*, 47(2) 163–74.

Schoen, D. (1987) *Educating the reflective practitioner*. San Francisco: Jossey-Bass.

Siskin, L.S. (1994) *Realms of Knowledge: Academic Departments in Secondary Schools*. London: Falmer.

Smith, R.G. (2007) Developing professional idealities and knowledge: becoming primary teachers, *Teachers and Teaching*, 13(4): 377–97.

Stenhouse, L. (1975) *An Introduction to Curriculum Research and Development*. London: Heinemann.

Training and Development Agency for Schools (TDA) (2007) *Professional Standards for Teachers*. London: TDA.

Van Manen, M. (1977) Linking ways of knowing with ways of being practical, *Curriculum Inquiry*, 6(3): 205–28.

2 Moving from reflective practitioner to practitioner researcher

Mike Ollerton

This chapter is about becoming a *practitioner researcher*. It will help you to:

- understand the importance of developing practitioner research skills as a set of processes designed to develop practice and *pedagogy*;
- find ways of systematically researching practice, recognizing how *reflective practice* relates to practitioner research;
- develop the art of *noticing-in-the-moment*;
- consider the gathering and use of *qualitative data* – how and from whom it might be collected;
- understand how to begin to analyse data.

Underpinning practitioner research is the knowledge that when we notice what our practice looks like then we can choose to continue and maintain or change that practice.

Researching into one's teaching

Teaching is a highly idiosyncratic craft. How you perceive yourself as a teacher is an important aspect of the development of *professional identity*, Campbell *et al.* (2004).

Practitioner research is about asking questions about how your teaching supports effective learning; this is at the heart of professional development. During daily contact with pupils, both inside and outside classrooms, you 'weigh up' situations and respond accordingly. You make decisions based upon knowledge gained from, and about, those you teach. You collect and process massive amounts of information that you act upon either in the future or during moment-by-moment interactions with pupils. Much of the information you collect is all part and parcel of being a teacher; it is incumbent upon you to use this information both to support pupils' academic and social development and to extend your professional expertise, '... curriculum research and development ought to belong to the teacher ...' Stenhouse (1975: 142); this issue of development needing to *belong to the teacher* is about ownership which relates to *teacher autonomy*.

The main difference between research being an incidental part of teaching and the teacher becoming an active practitioner researcher is intent. Research into practice requires a teacher to make intentional decisions to find out about the impact their teaching has upon pupils' learning. Research into practice requires the teacher to shift from gathering data incidentally and intuitively to gathering data in a determined and systematic way; thus the concept of *systematic enquiry* into practice.

One of the most exciting conceptual leaps I made as a teacher was to realize the power of finding out about myself as a teacher. I remember asking two fundamental questions. These were: 'Why teach?' and 'Why teach mathematics?' I did not realize at the time that by trying to find out about the 'why' I also learnt about the 'how'. How I taught and sought to cause pupils and adults to learn was an exciting journey ... and continues to be.

Noticing as a research paradigm and as a valuable teaching tool for developing pedagogy

We act upon what we notice, either consciously or subconsciously. Sometimes we may not be aware of the detail of what we notice and how this impacts on our actions. For example as a 'young' teacher when I wished to address the whole class I always asked pupils to 'put down your pens, pencils and anything else you have in your hands'. I became acutely aware of the detail of whether my request had been acted upon, yet I was blissfully unaware of why I felt pupils could not hear or take part in a discussion until they had emptied their hands. This is an example of making assumptions about how children learn, of not thinking through a recurrent event and the tension my request sometimes caused when one or another pupil decided to test out my resolve. Neither did I notice how ensuing interactions were more highly charged than they needed to be.

Only when I began to notice how such a request appeared to create a less than positive classroom atmosphere did I come to recognize that 'putting down a pencil' was not a necessary precursor for pupils to hear, think and partake in discussion. Noticing, therefore, became a valuable tool to enable me to make sense of and rationalize my teaching style.

The more I noticed events in my classroom, the more I chose to capture these events through reflective writing. The more reflective I became, the more I was able to make sense of what I saw, to explicitly rationalize where I was 'coming from' as a teacher; to explore and make sense of my developing pedagogy.

From reflective practitioner to practitioner researcher

Reflective practice is an important research tool in the practitioner researcher's tool box. One difference between reflective practitioner and practitioner researcher is the latter is a more deepening and systematic process. Reflecting upon practice is something we do as a matter of course – how a lesson went, how interactions with individuals or with a whole class panned out, what we would do differently on another occasion, how events from the previous lesson with a class informs planning for the next lesson with the class – these are natural ways to think about events. Writing about events is one way of helping evaluate what occurred. Seeking to understand why something occurred the way it did deepens the process of reflection, Ollerton (2004: 23). As we deepen our understanding of the power and the processes of reflection, Mason (2002: 15), we create opportunities to become more systematic enquirers or practitioner researchers. Opie (2004: 81) provides a useful list of key characteristics of practitioner researcher. For a definition I turn to Dadds:

> In its broadest sense, I take *practitioner research* to refer to forms of enquiry which people undertake in their own working contexts and, usually, on their own professional work, in whatever sphere they practice. The main purpose of the enquiry is to shed light on aspects of that work with a view to bringing about some benevolent change. (1998: 41)

Another difference between reflective practitioner and practitioner researcher lies in the *data analysis* subsequently carried out. Practitioner research requires a strong element of systematic data collection and analysis. Analysis serves to make the intuitive conscious and the implicit explicit. The more consciously explicit we become about our teaching, the more we are able to articulate pedagogy. Anecdotes provide examples of reflection into practice and are a valid, qualitative way of collecting data. The implications for the reader are to consider the following:

1   the importance of identifying a focus and beginning to gather data;
2   identifying other potential sources of data;
3   the value of collecting *qualitative data* and how *quantitative data* might be used;
4   analysing the data you collect.

I develop each of these below.

1 The importance of identifying a focus and beginning to gather data

To engage in practitioner researcher it is necessary to identify a focus. As you become clearer about what you intend to focus on you lessen the potential for your research becoming an amorphous mass of information that is neither systematically collected nor critically analysable. Altrichter *et al.* (1993: 33) pose the following two questions:

• 'What does a feasible starting point for action research look like?'
• 'How do teachers reach such starting points?'

Of course we may not begin with a clear focus but it is necessary to find a way of moving towards a focus; you can only begin to collect data in a systematic way when you know what you want to find out about. Finding a focus depends on what you are particularly interested in researching into (see Chapter 3 and 7 for further guidance). You may find a focus through discussion with others or through some off-the-cuff comment by a pupil. Often it can be useful to explore a particular tension within your teaching. The following is taken from 'Tensions' Mason (1988: 164): 'Have you ever found yourself talking, telling pupils things, and wished that somehow things were different, that *they* were doing the work?' Mason's question is fundamentally about who does the work in the classroom and focuses attention on the shift from teaching to learning.

If, for example, you become interested in developing effective ways of beginning a lesson, you might try to be particularly aware of what you notice about your own behaviour and your pupils' responses during the introductory part of a lesson. If you decide to collect data about the ways you plan and start lessons, you can write anecdotes of what transpired during several lesson beginnings. You might ask yourself some questions such as:

1 What processes did you go through as you planned some lesson beginnings?
2 What did you notice about how you felt during the beginning of these lessons?
3 What did you notice about how certain pupils responded during these lesson beginnings?

These questions are intended to create a framework for *noticing* both general and specific events. In turn, these noticings lead to written reflections. Noticing is an essential ingredient in the data-collection process. To notice minutiae, while you are in the throws of talking, listening, demonstrating, responding or modelling requires the teacher to develop the skill of *metacognition*. Prioritizing time after a lesson to make a brief note of anything you noticed; to capture what you were thinking about has the potential to be used as qualitative research data. Once you have turned these initial noticings into an anecdote the event becomes 'captured'. You can return to your anecdote days, weeks or even months later and, upon rereading, your writing will act as a trigger to remind you of what you did, how you felt and what you noticed about your pupils' responses.

2 Identifying other potential sources of data

The question to engage with here is: Where and from whom might I gather data?

Gathering data from other adults

As a trainee teacher there are inevitably going to be many occasions when another adult will be present in your classroom; your subject mentor, a support teacher, the generic mentor, a fellow trainee teacher, the class teacher, a head of department, your university tutor. All these people are potentially rich sources for providing you with valid data; particularly if you ask them to focus in detail on some aspect of the lesson you would value feedback on, such as your lesson beginnings. Asking them to provide written notes of their observations about how you taught and how certain pupils responded will provide information through another person's eyes. There are *ethical issues* here about being clear from the outset about why you are requesting such information and how you may wish to use it as data in the future. Ethical issues, however, are dealt with in Chapter 5; for now, at least, it is important to understand that ethical issues are omnipresent and must be considered whenever you ask someone else to provide data and, ultimately, help you with your research.

Gathering data from pupils

Pupils can provide an incredibly rich source of data and ethical issues similarly abound. Asking pupils for feedback, however, on how they experienced your teaching is, indeed, a 'shark-infested' pan of custard. As an example I recently asked a group of KS2 pupils to write a brief statement about how they had felt about a lesson I had taught. As I read through their comments I was pleased with the positive nature of what many pupils had written, until I came across one comment that read *'It was boring'*. This obviously presented me with the issue of both *why* this comment appeared and *how* this comment informed my planning for the next lesson with the same group.

Issues of *validity* and *reliability* figure in the research recipe here; again these issues are dealt with in Chapter 6. If you are going to ask pupils to provide feedback, then it is important to be very clear about what you are asking them to give feedback on and why you are asking them for information. You need to prepare yourself for what might potentially be disconcerting comments and you also need to recognize the opposite effect, of being told just what you want to hear ... that is, you are the best teacher they have ever had and they wish that you taught them all the time! *Ethically* you must gain permission from pupils if you intend to use their data for your research project.

Below is another example of what can happen when we ask pupils for data. The context was a consideration of whether the amount of noise, emanating from discussion in the classroom, was conducive to effective learning. The following short piece of writing emerged from an incidental conversation with a secondary pupil who was keen to talk about her experience of discussion in one of her classrooms.

Case Study 1

My maths teacher likes to be in complete control of a class. This is understandable to a certain degree, but he forbids us to talk unless specified other wise. Now this is ok, when he says 'I'd like no talking during this test', obviously this is fine, but then he takes it too far and won't let us talk full stop. At the beginning of an exercise, say from a text book usually, he will say, 'no talking, I want to hear you concentrating'. This I find extremely annoying. I sit with two boys on a desk for three, and we are all great friends. We have a really good time together, talking about maths or not. I've known Joe and Jamie since year 7, so roughly 3 years, and I have sat next to Joe for all of them. If one of us is stuck or just generally has a problem we will always help each other. When Jamie joined our table, we became a trio and discussed things together. Is this scary?

Reflection on Case Study 1

There is a significant issue here about using this piece of writing. Because this data is about another teacher's practice, it leads me to an ethical dilemma. Do I use this data as a powerful example of pupil voice? Obviously I have done so in the knowledge that the pupil, the teacher nor the school can be identified.

As a practitioner researcher, however, and to be consistent with Dadd's definition, your research must fundamentally be an enquiry into your practice.

There are five important aspects of asking pupils to provide you with data, which are:

1 being clear to your pupils about why you are asking them for information;
2 being clear about what, specifically, you are asking them to give you feedback on;
3 posing questions so pupils can tell you things you may not necessarily expect to hear;
4 considering the pros and cons of trust and anonymity;
5 'pupil voice' is potentially a powerful way of developing a valuable learning culture within a classroom and across a school.

Point 4 relates to how pupils might tell you different things if they think there may be some comeback and may feel more comfortable to remain anonymous. Alternatively, and in order to deepen your research, you may wish to follow up some of their comments so it would be useful to know who has written what. One way through this minefield is to offer pupils the choice of remaining anonymous or not; explaining that if they choose to add their name to their comment you might wish to discuss some of the issues raised in greater depth.

As such, by involving pupils to help you become a more effective teacher sets the scene for honest and open professional relationships between teacher and pupils. This resonates with the mantra 'a reflective teacher is an effective teacher'. However, we must always be careful of uncritically accepting or believing mantras ... for example, 'Don't smile till Christmas ...' The point I seek to make here is the reason for engaging with research into practice is to improve practice by developing pedagogy. However, for research into practice to become an effective vehicle for professional development, we must reflect in a systematic way and subsequently analyse what the information tells us about our teaching. Without depth of *critical analysis* our reflections are in danger of becoming a paper exercise ... you know the kind of garbage we fill up files with in order to jump through certain teacher training hoops; jumping off this particular soap-box I shall move on.

3 The value of qualitative data and how quantitative data might be used

I do not intend to engage in any depth with the qualitative versus quantitative data argument because there is value in both approaches depending on the nature of the research being carried out. However, teaching is a highly personal and individual craft and is riven with subjectivity; what works well for one teacher does not guarantee similar success for another. As far as practitioner research goes using quantitative research methods to seek to demonstrate objectifiable statistical significance has little to offer a teacher who is engaged in passionate enquiry (Dadds 1995).

The main reason for engaging with number-crunching, when carrying out practitioner research, is to look for trends in the data in terms of which issues arise more frequently. Returning to research into lesson beginnings, if you gain data from a) your reflections, b) other adults and c) pupils some of which indicate, for example, your tendency to answer your own questions during a lesson beginning, this provides information about your teaching style. You may wish, therefore, to explore this phenomenon further. You might then trawl the data for other trends to see what the data is telling you. This is touching upon data analysis that I develop below.

The main reason for using qualitative data is that it can be gathered from different sources in a variety of ways. In Table 2.1 I list potential data sources and possible methods we might use to gather it.

Table 2.1 Potential data sources

Potential data sources	How data might be gathered
Self	Scribbled notes from events noticed in-the-moment
Self	Brief reflective notes written after a lesson
Self	Substantive anecdotes
Other adults	A write-up of a lesson you have taught
Other adults	Brief notes of casual observations
Other adults	Notes arising from discussions with yourself
Pupils	Questionnaire
Pupils	Asking pupils to write one or two paragraphs about a specific aspect of your teaching
Pupils	Giving each pupil a Post-it note and asking them to write one thing they like about and one thing they think could be improved about your teaching
Pupils	Asking pupils to write a note arising from discussions with a voluntary group

If you are to engage in systematic data collection it is important to have a range of sources and methods of collecting data; this connects with *triangulation*, which is discussed in Chapters 9 and 10.

4 Analysing the data you collect

Condensing and *clumping* are two of the processes you can engage with to analyse data. Condensing data is a process of reading through the information you have gathered, in whatever form it has been collected, and seeking to name or to classify specific issues that emerge. For example, issues that might arise during lesson beginnings might be about:

1 how you plan to have all your resources to hand;
2 how you gain pupils' attention;
3 deciding upon strategies to engage pupils in initial discussions;
4 considering which strategies you use (hopefully beyond 'hands up') to encourage responses and participation by pupils;
5 how long you are able to maintain pupils' concentration before moving on to another phase of the lesson (hopefully where the pupils 'do' the work).

Using the above list I might name, condense or categorize them as:

1 resources;
2 gaining attention;
3 discussion strategies;
4 encouraging participation;
5 maintaining attention.

While issues such as these are inevitably interconnected, they can also stand alone in terms of perceiving them as specific events framed within a lesson beginning.

Once you have begun to collect a list of categories you can assign specific comments from the data to them. As you keep reading through your data you are likely to add other categories and you are also likely to clump categories together. So, for instance, where you initially thought that organizing discussion strategies and encouraging participation were two different types of issues, you may decide 'discussion' is a subset of a larger category, namely 'participation'. What you are doing, therefore, is engaging with processes of review and refinement; continually seeking to make sense of what the data reveals. This is discussed further in Chapter 10.

An example of collecting data through an anecdote, subsequent analysis and making sense of pedagogy

To conclude this chapter I offer an example of writing an anecdote about noticing-in-the-moment. I present some analysis arising from the anecdote and finish with a discussion of what this analysis informs me about my pedagogy.

I wrote the anecdote nearly 20 years ago about an event with a Year 7 class.

Case Study 2

With my Y7 mathematics class I had been working on the notion of 'stuckness' in terms of wanting pupils not to be afraid of being stuck on a problem and instead to see this as a useful part of learning mathematics. I had subsequently posed the class a problem to explore and a request that if they felt stuck to go through a sequence of steps before turning to me for help. This sequence was a) to try to see for themselves what they were stuck on, b) to ask a friend for help and c) to ask me for help.

> Twenty or so minutes into the lesson Jemma came to me and announced 'I am stuck!' I immediately held out my hand, shook hers and said 'Hello Stuck, I am Mr Ollerton'. Jemma laughed and we proceeded to discuss the nature of her stuckness. Later in the lesson Jemma approached me again and I said 'Hello Stuck'. Quick as you like Jemma responded 'I'm not Stuck, I'm Unstuck!' We both laughed and I chose to publicly celebrate Jemma's comment.

Reflection on Case Study 2

The reason I remember this event is because I wrote it down later that evening. At first I speedily wrote an account, just enough to remind me of the context and to capture the sequence of events. At the time I only had a vague sense this was an interesting event; it was not until I analysed the event later I gained a fuller understanding of the value of my actions.

Later I added more detail to the anecdote and later still I analysed the anecdote to reveal to myself aspects of pedagogy. My analysis revealed the following:

1 I believed that helping pupils become conscious of being stuck should not be seen as a 'bad thing' and had a positive impact upon learning.
2 Being explicit with pupils about what strategies they might use when they felt stuck would help some pupils overcome the fear some had about mathematics.
3 Working with *mixed-attainment groups* (from Year 7 to Year 11) meant engaging pupils with the processes of exploration to support their differentiated states as learners of mathematics.
4 Taking an opportunity to engage in an amusing way with one pupil enhanced my relationship with her.
5 I became more explicitly aware of the kind of atmosphere I wished to create in my classroom, thus deciding to explain what had happened to the rest of the class became part of my desire to be honest and open and to celebrate such events.

These five points describe what became intuitive, implicit values; my pedagogy. Of course the third point contains 'massive' pedagogic issues about choosing not to label pupils and the importance of learning through exploration.

Looking at and exploring aspects of our teaching we may wish to enquire into; to explicitly develop one's *pedagogy* is professionally empowering. Collecting information and using such information to develop practice is the basis of practitioner research. Practitioner research is a tool for understanding the pedagogy that underpins our practices and simultaneously helps us make some sense of how children learn.

Glossary

clumping (data)   putting similar types of information together as the initial part of the process of analysis.
condensing (data)   classifying or naming information about a common issue.
critical analysis   searching and researching through data; looking deeper into data in order to make sense of what the data is telling us. Looking systematically at data in order to get beneath the surface.

data analysis   looking into and making sense of information gathered for purposes of research.

ethical issues   an agreed code by which professionals carry out their work in order to maintain personal integrity and to protect the rights of others, both emotionally and professionally.

metacognition   being able to see the minutia while still being aware of wider events. Also see *noticing*.
mixed-attainment groups   a moral and ethical way of grouping schoolchildren thus avoiding a form of educational apartheid.

noticing (or noticing-in-the-moment)   developing one's awareness to become sensitive to unanticipated events taking place.

pedagogy   the underpinning educational principles that inform and shape practice.
practitioner research   enquiry; the art of studying own practice.
practitioner researcher   someone who studies or enquires into their practice.
professional identity   aspects of our work life that we give value to and wish to be associated with.

qualitative data   information gathered about feelings and perceptions of certain events; data cannot be measured on a scale and is subjective rather than objectifiable.

quantitative data   information that can be measured on an agreed scale. If two researchers gathered the same data, using the same scale of measure, the results should be identical.

reflective practice   a subset of practitioner research; systematic consideration of one's teaching and students' learning.

reliability (of data)   this refers to the way data has been collected, with regard to the intrinsic truth value of data. Those providing data must do so of their own free will and must understand the reasons for providing the researcher with data.

research paradigm   classifying or identifying approaches in order to enquire into, find out about or delve into.

systematic enquiry   finding out about something in ordered, considered and rational ways.

triangulation (of data)   gathering information from more than two sources, about a common event in order to look into a specific phenomenon.

teacher autonomy   decisions and actions teachers make and take that are of a teacher's own volition.

validity (of data)   seeking to ensure that collected data has not been skewed or gratuitously 'fixed', for example not giving all the children a lolly prior to asking them what they thought of your lesson!

References and further reading

Altrichter, H., Posch, P. and Somekh, B. (1993) *Teachers Investigate their Work*. London: Routledge.

Campbell, A., McNamara, O. and Gilroy, P. (2004) *Practitioner Research and Professional Development in Education*. London: Paul Chapman Publishing.

Dadds, M. (1995) *Passionate Enquiry*. London: Falmer Press.

Dadds, M. (1998) Supporting practitioner research, *Educational Action Research*, 6(1): 39–52.

Mason, J. (1988) *Tensions*, in D. Pimm (ed.) *Mathematics, Teachers and Children*. London: Hodder and Stoughton in association with the Open University.

Mason, J. (2002) *Researching your Own Practice: The Discipline of Noticing*. London: Routledge Falmer.

Ollerton, M. (2004) *Creating Positive Classrooms*. London: Continuum.

Opie, C. (2004) *Doing Educational Research*. London: Sage Publications.

Stenhouse, L. (1975) *An Introduction to Curriculum Research and Development*. London: Heinemann.

Part II   Getting started

3 Survival skills

Sarah Hall and Ruth Jones

Learning can be a struggle but it is one that is worthwhile. We would not be so well informed without people who were prepared to devote time and effort to broadening not only their own but also our understanding of teaching and learning. Undertaking classroom-based research is difficult, particularly when you are working full time. It is daunting and exhausting. However, if you believe it is valuable then you will have the determination and self-discipline necessary to succeed.

> If you don't know where you are going every road will get you nowhere.
>
> (Henry Kissinger)

It may seem a strange place to begin but you must have some idea of what you are going to produce at the end of the research project. If you know where you are heading the journey will be much easier. You may know what you want to research but for many choosing a topic can be problematic. You may have an interest in a certain area of education and your research focus can be further developed through relevant reading and research. As you become more informed you will find your interest becomes more focused. It is beneficial to keep your research focus simple for if the topic is too ambitious you will quickly become overwhelmed (see Chapters 2 and 7). One of the main purposes of classroom-based research is your own educational development: you will learn, or improve, skills of research, discussion, justification of your decisions, data collection, and the analysis and evaluation of your research conclusions. You will probably have to accept that after all your hard work what you produce may not be ground breaking: however, you will have learnt valuable transferable skills, including independent research and educational analysis.

Case Study 1: Ruth Jones

My research has always risen from dilemmas. As an early years' teacher I was torn between the head teacher's suggestions that in order to prepare children for Year 1 I should have them sitting down every afternoon completing handwriting and maths, and my belief, that children learn best through play. This dilemma had a huge impact on me and made me question my practice.

I found myself thinking more and more about children's learning particularly in maths and it was this dilemma that triggered my research as I began to wonder whether I had the balance right: were too many activities teacher-directed or, on the other hand, were there too many child-initiated activities? What were the children learning in either situation if anything?

Reflection on Case Study 1

The classroom before the research

Young children are physically active. As a teacher I never had them sitting down for extended periods of time but I began to consider whether the head teacher had a point and I should. Was I preparing the children in the right manner for the Key Stage 1 classroom where many activities are teacher-directed and there is little learning through play? Moreover, I was aware of the different philosophy of other classroom practitioners within the school who operated on a much more formal basis. There was definitely a conflict in my school and I was confused about the best way forward. It was this dilemma that triggered my classroom-based research.

Development of the research question

As I reflected on my practice in the light of recent research, I refined my research focus. I wanted to explore what children enjoyed, their definitions of play and work, and their awareness of their learning. I also considered my own and other educators' definitions of play and work.

I read widely and found the situation was complex: scholarly research on this issue was broad-ranging and often conflicting. It is no wonder so many of us are unsure of what effective pedagogy for the early years actually looks like particularly when we are being encouraged to subject young children to teaching and learning approaches that are more appropriate for older learners.

My methodology

I undertook data collection over a three-week period. My methodology involved three elements:

1 observation;
2 oral questionnaires;
3 triangulation.

Reception children were observed undertaking specific mathematical tasks for one minute prior to being given an oral questionnaire. The activities used in the study were ones I already use: they had a play element and some were open-ended. I narrowed my observations to those activities that were teacher-directed for several reasons; I wondered whether the children would recognize the play element in the tasks and I was constrained by time. Children were asked the following questions:

- Are you playing or working?
- Are you happy or sad?
- Why are you happy or sad?
- What are you learning about?

The adult acted as scribe. The questions were short and simple as I did not want to 'interrogate' the children. I endeavoured to ensure each child could not hear what others were saying in order to minimize repeated answers. Initially, children were asked to choose either a happy or sad face to show how they felt about an activity. This became unnecessary after the first few occasions as children were confident to simply say how they felt. I did wonder about the reliability of these answers as children may have been trying to please by saying the activities made them feel happy.

Children were also asked the following questions about work and play:

- What do you like playing with at school?
- What is play?
- What do you like working with at school?
- What is work?
- Can you think of a time when you were playing and working at the same time?

The results obtained from both questionnaires were quantitative and could be expressed as simple ratios. Complex statistical analysis was not appropriate with such a small number of participants (see Chapters 6 and 7).

My teaching assistant, the Key Stage 1 teacher and the head teacher, were approached and asked to give their interpretations as to what they regarded as 'play' and what they regarded as 'work'. Themes were allowed to be generated by the data with as few preconceptions as possible. These themes were coded until the essence of the data was exposed. It was hoped that by these methods insight could be obtained into the way children perceived the difference between play and work, and if there was any profound difference with that of an adult's interpretation.

Observing children is an important part of my job; it is how I plan and provide learning opportunities for them so I did not envisage any ethical dilemmas with this research. Furthermore, I did not envisage any problems in conducting this research as it was close to my normal practice. The difference was that the observations and record-keeping were more systematic. Children were told we would be asking questions about what they were doing and what they thought so we could find out how to make teaching and learning better. There was no discrimination as all reception children were involved equally.

My methods produced a great deal of enlightening data. Children and adults agreed that play involves role play, using toys and choice, while work relates to literacy and numeracy. Children who enjoyed an activity would usually still consider it to be work if it had been adult-directed. Children's understanding of learning objectives was often different to my own; however, theirs were usually sensible alternatives. There was not time in this study to question children while they were involved in activities they would consider to be play. I am planning to do this in the future; as I have already stated I am a reflective practitioner and understand that if we are to take the child's growth seriously and make our own jobs more interesting this needs to be undertaken.

Conclusions

This study made me appreciate why perceptions of play and work are so hotly debated. The claims made by researchers can be difficult to assess unless you know exactly where they are coming from. By gaining a greater understanding of my practice, the children I teach benefited, and as my research also involved my teaching assistant, opportunities to discuss issues and philosophies have since emerged; this has had a positive effect on her professional development and the classroom learning environment.

A comment about sitting children down every afternoon to prepare them for their KS1 classroom was the trigger that started this research. Mason (2002) refers to what triggers a new phase of personal development as 'some form of disturbance', and it was certainly that. Perhaps most importantly I have come to know what I already knew. The definitions of play and work are not what are important in the classroom. It is providing children with appropriate and enjoyable experiences to enhance learning.

Case Study 2: Sarah Hall

> *'How can levelled assessment be practically introduced into the classroom context in accordance with assessment for, and assessment of, learning principles?'*
>
> I completed my first piece of 'formal' classroom-based research during my PGCE training. Here I hope to share with you some brief, but hopefully useful, survival skills based on my own experiences. During your teaching practice you will constantly be involved in 'informal' classroom research as teaching, by its very nature, involves constant trialling of new ideas, review and readjustment. However, starting 'formal' research can be daunting.
>
> The essence of classroom-based research, that it is independent and organic, is, on the one hand, that which makes it relevant and of the moment, but on the other hand, intimidating – the fact you may have no set direction, or a research title from a third party can be initially unsettling. My advice is to start off your research embracing rather than fearing this freedom – you are only limited in what you do by your own creativity and imagination. You must, however, remember that the person doing the research, you, is also the person who will be teaching – this has the positive result that your findings can be applied directly to your own practice, but it also means that you must from the start set *realistic* goals. Finally, remember that although you may be undertaking individual research, you are ultimately a part of a much wider network of teachers and learners, so do not be afraid to ask for help; take constructive advice and share your own good practice on classroom-based research.
>
> This research was carried out within the Religious Studies department of a large 11–18 comprehensive school following

consultation with the Head of Department and an analysis of departmental development needs.

To begin, I researched levelled assessment requirements and strategies from both an academic and classroom-based perspective, including organizing meetings with Religious Studies departments in other schools to discuss their levelling strategies and tasks. I set myself a realistic time limit for this period of research (given the pressures of teacher training) and consciously focused on 'practical' strategies that could be adopted within the classroom context. Remember, you are conducting a piece of active research that will impact on the classroom rather than writing an academic tome.

The next step, given time and practical constraints, was to 'hone in' on a specific research task. I decided to focus on the development and evaluation of pupil-friendly proformas for use with KS3 levelled assessment, specifically

1) a generic 'pupil-friendly' level descriptor,
2) a pupil self-assessment sheet to be used when completing a levelled assessment and
3) an attainment progress tracker for use throughout the academic year.

The objective of the research was to develop 'generic' proformas that would be pupil-friendly and staff-friendly. I opted to approach research through a 'pupil panel' – who better to offer first-hand evaluation of pupil-friendly assessment solutions than pupils themselves! I developed a selection of 'models' for each proforma and invited pupils from a selection of age and ability ranges to join the pupil panel that met over a series of lunch-times. Via a cyclical process of group discussion and adaptation of each model, and the completion of individual pupil questionnaires and evaluation forms, a 'perfect' proforma for each of the three areas of research was created. I then trialled the proformas within the classroom and, following further pupil feedback, ironed out any remaining chinks. The proforma models were then presented and discussed at a staff meeting and to my surprise were not only adopted by the department for the next academic year but also filtered into the whole school assessment policy.

My aim in undertaking the research was not to create the 'perfect proforma', but rather to create 'organic working models', which could be adapted and changed as staff and pupils worked with them. School-based research is a fluid activity and the results you achieve should not, and will not, be static. It is this dynamic element of school-based research that makes it approachable no matter what level of 'teacher' you are, and that also enables 'you' as 'a researcher' to be both an active learner and self-reflective practitioner. Keep your research realistic and achievable; it is far easier to increase your research field of enquiry than try and reduce it once you have started. Moreover, projects do not have to be ground breaking to have a big impact on your own personal development and that of your classroom, department and possibly school.

Reflection on Case Study 2

Completing school-based research

Throughout the research process you will need to remain focused on realistic research aims and objectives and adopt a pragmatic planning and research strategy. Above all, you must know when to stop even if your end result is not that which you originally intended. Yes, there will be more that you could do; there always will be, but that can always form the basis of another project.

Classroom-based research, by its very nature, takes a different format to more traditional research systems, and you may find, as I did, that the adaptation of an action research cycle proves beneficial in focusing your research and results writing. Action research is basically a continual cyclical process of the collection of, and analysis of, data followed by a refocus of research question. Hypotheses are made, researched, refocused and researched again in a systematic but active fashion. This type of research provides an enormous opportunity for you, as a classroom practitioner, to focus on matters of educational priority while developing your own professional practice in a systematic manner. As it enables holistic research to be carried out within specific and real contexts, the emphasis is on *testing* research questions (whatever the results) and *developing practice* rather than reaching definitive solutions; this is what makes this type of research approachable and highly applicable to all teachers, no matter what stage of their career. Research is an open-ended and active learning process.

You will need to begin your research with a research problem – start to think about what contradictions exist between what is currently happening in the classroom and what you want to happen? (See Chapters 2 and 7). You could focus on a problem that you are aware of, you could have an idea which you would like to try out, or you could just have a general notion that through your research you may be able to improve something. The aim of school-based research is not to find the answer to the ultimate question of life, the universe and everything, but rather to offer a way of approaching a problem and perhaps facilitating transition. Most importantly the research problem should be something that you, as researcher, are interested in if you are going to be completing this alongside teaching, possible study commitments and attempting to also remain sane.

A very simple plan of attack

Organization, organization, organization

- Even if you find plans unhelpful, planning is indispensable for this type of work especially if you are formally writing up your research. Create a hard or computer file in which you have clear subsections relating to your research; keep clear notes of all books, websites, journals read, keep copies of any draft workings, interviews, questionnaires and so on for your appendix. If you are mentally organized it really does make the whole process much easier.

Create a research timeframe

- Although this is difficult to do when you do not know what exactly you are focusing on, creating a general timeframe where you can assign time periods to initial 'academic' research, carrying out research and writing up of results will help you to focus your project and also ensure that it remains manageable. As classroom-based research demands a continual zigzag process of review and readjustment, your timeframe will be fluid rather than static. I would suggest allowing small adjustments to the overall time limits of your research if needed, but ultimately use the timeframe as a means of controlling what you do – if you cannot do it in the time you have allowed yourself then leave it out. Research should not be an unwelcome burden on your teaching, studying or free time.

Identify a research area

- This may start off being general or specific. What is important is that you can quickly narrow the scope of your research to one explicit area in order to make the project manageable. Remember this type of research is likely to be open-ended so do not panic if you do not know the 'direction' your research may take you in.
- Start off small – your research can always grow in other directions but take on too much and it can engulf you and you will lose

motivation and focus. Resist the urge to do everything. In the case study, I initially started off just researching pupil-friendly level descriptors, the other two elements of the research I adopted later when I was comfortable with the research workload and time commitments.

- Do thorough but realistic background research – researching your 'area' in government documents, academic books and the web may help you to refocus your research area and narrow your field of enquiry further. Ensure you spend some time investigating current provision in this area and asking yourself what you can feasibly do given your limitations. Your research does not have to be radical; it can build upon the work of others, perhaps even something that has already been undertaken at school. Remember, classroom-based research is a cyclical process of research, refocus and research.

- Be a bit selfish; ask yourself how completing this research could benefit you as a classroom practitioner? Although sharing of good practice must be undertaken, if you put time and effort into research it will benefit you whether it be with classroom confidence, insight into classroom practices, motivation or career progression. The case study research gave me self-assurance in an area that was still relatively new to Religious Studies specialists and was something that definitely aided me come my first teaching interview and first year of teaching practice.

Devise a research hypothesis

- Ask yourself how the theoretical background you have been researching can be put into common-sense practice. Remember that this should be a working title that is flexible to change and adapt as you work through the process of research, refocus and further research. Nevertheless, the importance of the research hypothesis is that it acts as a mental focus. I had a large copy of my hypothesis on the office wall as a sort of mantra – it kept me focused and aided me to resist the temptation to go down blind, albeit possibly exciting, avenues of further research.

Choose a suitable research methodology/methodologies

- Each research project is unique and as such the methodology you choose to adopt will also be unique – there is no right or wrong method. However, it is useful to draw on a combination of complementary methods to gain a more complete research picture, and if possible use both open-ended and closed methods along with qualitative and quantative data. In the case study I used many methodologies including individual interviews, group interviews, a diary record, observation, pupil voice and in situ questionnaires. Although you may initially feel hesitant using open-ended methods as you are not in control, they do allow for flexibility of response and may lead you to discover something unexpected!

- Be aware of the limitations and strengths of each methodology and its impact on your research, especially if you are writing up your project. Do not be afraid, however, of 'trial and error' as this is a constructive learning process.
- Use pupils and pupil voice where possible, especially as your research will undoubtedly have an impact on the classroom.
- Remember to ensure that your methodology is ethically sound and you have followed university or school guidelines – if in doubt ask before you start your research.

Complete your research and write-up of results

If you have kept an organized file of research and workings this part of the research should be fairly straightforward. It will also provide you with an opportunity to reflect on what you have learnt from the process of research and to dialogue about new questions that have emerged from research (see Chapters 11 and 12).

Survival steps

- Have a realistic plan and timeframe for the research – break tasks into do-able actions that you can achieve within work and study commitments.
- Remember that you are not trying to solve something but rather that your research is active, fluid and organic.
- Accept that there are limitations to the research process.
- If something does not do what you originally planned, it does not mean that it is useless, but rather use this constructively in your learning processes.

How school-based research can aid your early teaching practice

It can be difficult being a new teacher in any school; however, do not allow the fact that you are new or an NQT to stop you discussing with your line manager the possibility of undertaking a small-scale 'formal' classroom-based research project. Look at the departmental or school improvement plan and see if there is an area that could be looked at within your classroom. If you fear 'treading on toes' then complete something that will have an impact on *you* as a new teacher within *your* own classroom. Do stress that carrying out research in no way suggests the inadequacy of current policies or practices, but rather is something that will inform your own teaching practice and that acts as relevant continuous professional development (CPD) (see Chapter 13).

Completing classroom-based research will show that you have enthusiasm, and a commitment and responsibility towards your own learning and professional development (see Chapter 13). As you will have first-hand involvement with researching and implementing classroom policies and practices, your confidence, resilience, innovation and communication skills will increase. As a self-reflective practitioner you will be able to adapt practices for the benefit of teaching, learning and behaviour and ensure that opportunities are provided for all to achieve their potential. You cannot underestimate how much this process of 'self-reflectiveness', which comes to the fore through classroom-based research, will have a positive impact on your teaching career – the ability to reflect, re-evaluate practices and reflect again ensures excellent classroom practice (see Chapters 2 and 13).

Finally, I hope that you look upon completing research as an opportunity rather than a chore: an opportunity to become a more focused practitioner who demonstrates, through good practice, a passion for classroom learning.

Reference

Mason, J. (2002) *Researching Your Own Practice: The Discipline of Noticing*. London and New York: Routledge Falmer.

4   Information skills for classroom research

James Fraser and Hannah Hough

Introduction

This chapter introduces you to helpful strategies that will enable you to *identify*, *locate*, *evaluate* and *utilize* appropriate information for doing classroom research quickly and easily.

As student teachers you are increasingly expected to engage with critical research and reflective practice in the classroom. You can benefit greatly by applying practical information skills to help cope with these demands.

Information skills is more than just being able to use technology to find information; it is about making choices concerning the different kinds of information available and about being discerning and evaluative in the whole research process.

The aim of the chapter is to guide you through a series of progressive steps that will provide a structured approach to good information skills practice. This will help to demystify the often overwhelming and intimidating range of information sources and tools that are now available to you.

The chapter offers you advice on how to find high-quality information effectively with an awareness of the tight timeframes that you often work within. It is also important that if working at M level you are critically aware of the varying quality of information and feel confident to evaluate the appropriateness of what you find.

Section 1: Identifying the required information

This section will help you:

- know how to identify required information;
- access the appropriate resources;
- utilize the most effective tools for your information need.

There is a vast amount of information available to you and it is increasing all the time. It may seem intimidating when you first begin your research to be faced with so much scope and so many options. This section will help you to begin the information-gathering process in an organized way, selecting the types of information you require and working out how to search effectively and find it.

Know how to identify what kind of information you might need

Here are some questions that you can ask yourself in the first instance to try and determine what kind of information you need to fulfil your research needs:

- Do you need information that is *up-to-date* or *historical*? Perhaps a mix of both?
- Do you need facts, statistics, results, original artworks, letters? *Primary information* can provide a direct insight into an event because the information has not been rewritten or revised.
- Are you more interested in the perceptions and uses of primary information? *Secondary information* has been modified or arranged for a specific purpose, for example summaries, overviews, critiques, analyses, evaluations. This information may be biased by an author's opinion, but can provide a quick way of seeing an overview or viewpoint of a topic.
- Do you want *practical evidence*, for example the results of a research project or a case study? Or perhaps you utilize *theoretical ideas* for your work, for example new theories and models within the area of your studies?
- Do you need *scholarly information* that is assessed for quality before it is published to make sure that the content is accurate, for example research articles (which are peer-reviewed, see Chapters 11 and 12)? Or do you need *popular information* that is released without any quality checks, but can be useful for researching popular opinions, for example opinion polls or magazine articles?
- Do you need collections of information, summaries of facts, brief definitions, for example encyclopaedic definitions? *Tertiary information* is often published a long time after the event has

happened and briefly summarizes all the information for a specific event.

Know which resources hold the information you need

Once you have identified what kind of information you need, the next step is to determine what resources will provide you with that information. The following list will help you in this process:

- *Audio recordings and podcasts* can contain useful *primary information* such as interviews, but may be quite difficult to find within some disciplines.
- *Books/eBooks* are the obvious starting point for all kinds of *secondary information* such as *practical, theoretical, popular* and *tertiary*.
- *CD-ROMs* are not as widely used as they once were but they can often provide useful information, for example *statistics*.
- *Conference papers* can provide you with very *up-to-date* and *scholarly* information.
- *Journals/eJournals* are extremely useful for *up-to-date, practical, theoretical* and *scholarly* information.
- *Newspapers* are useful for *up-to-date* and *popular* information.
- *Theses* are works written for higher-level degrees (Masters and PhD) and can be useful for *up-to-date, scholarly* and *theoretical* information.
- *Videos/DVDs/TV programmes* can provide *up-to-date, scholarly, practical, primary, secondary* and *popular* information.
- *Websites* can provide all the different kinds of information for education including government websites and standards agencies, but generally information quality on the Internet is a big issue and this will be discussed in depth in section 3 of this chapter.

Know which tools can be used to locate relevant resources

There are a wide variety of tools that you can use to access the resources mentioned above. It is very important that you ask your library what tools they subscribe to as not all libraries offer the same resources. The list below is an indicative selection of tools that you will find useful for locating your desired information:

Library catalogues for books, teaching materials, newspapers and journals

Your library catalogue contains information about all the resources that are held in the library. You can search for titles, authors, keywords and numbers. You *cannot* normally search for journal articles or chapters of books.

Indexing databases for journal articles, theses and conference proceedings

Indexing databases (also called bibliographic databases) hold bibliographic information about journal articles and conference proceedings. They are very useful if you want to identify articles and papers about a specific subject and can be searched easily for article titles or authors. They do not hold the full text of the indexed items, but include information on a wide range of different topics. Examples include:

- AEI (Australian Education Index);
- BEI (British Education Index);
- Index to theses.

Full-text databases for full text journal articles

Full-text databases are similar to indexing databases, except they allow you to find whole articles online, rather than just bibliographic information about the articles. This means that you do not need to go to the library to collect the materials; you can access them immediately from your computer. These tools do, however, only hold information about a small number of resources; therefore your search results may be limited. Examples include:

- Education-line;
- Professional Development Collection.

Search engines for web pages and files off the Internet

Web search engines allow you to search the web for web pages and documents. A web search engine only searches a small proportion of the total web. Different search engines search different sections of the web, therefore you may want to use more than one search engine or use a *metasearch* engine that can search many smaller engines at once (although not to the same degree of accuracy). Examples include:

- Google: www.google.com is a very popular search engine, has advanced search available and there is also a 'Google Scholar' search engine for academic papers (www.scholar.google.com)

- MetaCrawler: www.metacrawler.com is an example of a meta-search engine.

Information gateways for quality-assured web pages

Information gateways hold information on a specific subject area. Quality web resources on a specific subject are selected by trained staff and are compiled into listings of useful resources for you to search or browse. Examples include:

- Intute: www.intute.ac.uk is a free online service providing access to web resources for education and research.

Alert services and current awareness tools for the very latest information in academic research

You could use current awareness tools when you are undertaking large research projects and need to know everything that is currently understood on a specific subject. Some current awareness tools allow you to search unpublished/pre-print papers, and others can let you search for research that is currently in progress.

Most indexing and full-text databases as well as information gateways will have a current awareness feature.

Section 2: Searching skills

This section will help you to:

- identify, expand, refine and combine your keywords;
- use search techniques to limit your searches;
- maintain a record of your completed searches.

Searching for information can be a complicated process. As you have seen in the previous section there is a large amount of information available, many places to look for it and all sorts of different search tools available. This section will help you to find relevant information efficiently and effectively.

Keywords

The most important part of the searching process is choosing your keywords. Electronic tools such as databases and search engines will only search for the exact words that you provide, so it is important that you are equipped with a range of defining and descriptive keywords to make sure that you cover all the elements of the research topic and that you do not miss out on important information due to alternative ways of expressing your search terms. Remember that you are in control of your searching, not the computer!

A very effective way to begin to gather your keywords is to use techniques such as mind-mapping. Mind-maps can help you to:

- identify major concepts of the topic;
- think about these concepts in detail;
- decide which concepts are of most interest;
- find out which concepts are least clear;
- break concepts down into small details and ideas;
- generate keywords.

Figure 4.1 shows an example of how a *mind-map* might be used. Once you have identified your key areas for investigation you will need to think of synonyms, alternative spellings and singular and plural forms for each of the main terms, and consider broader and narrower ways of expressing the topic by trying them in turn:

- *Synonyms* are 'like' words, for example 'teacher' or 'educator' or 'lecturer'.

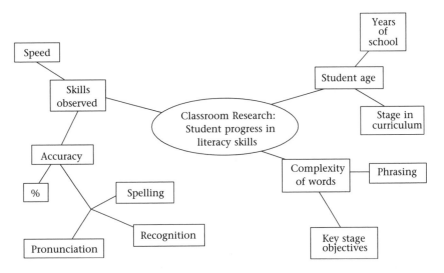

Figure 4.1: Mind-map

- 'Education' is a broader term than 'teaching'.
- Check for alternative spellings, for example organisation or organization.
- The keyword 'teach' can be pluralized and expanded, for example teaches, teaching, teacher, and so on.

Search techniques

Nearly all databases allow you to refine your search by using techniques of some kind to make it easier for you to retrieve helpful results when keyword searching. The following are the most frequently offered, but using the Help function in whichever database you are searching will give you much fuller information about constructing complex searches.

Boolean operators

Combining your keywords is crucial to find what you are looking for. Boolean operators allow you to combine your keywords in ways that give you control over your searching.

Boolean searching at its most basic involves the use of **AND** and **OR** to define the relationships between words.

- The use of **AND** will narrow a search to make it more specific: the records retrieved must contain *both* search words, for example EDUCATION **AND** ART.
- The use of **OR** will widen a search and will combine your synonyms: the records retrieved may contain *either* or *both* search words, for example TEACHER **OR** EDUCATOR.

Truncation or wild cards

Truncation symbols, or wild cards, are used to replace one or more letters in order to retrieve different forms of a search word. The symbols used are usually ? or *, for example TEACH* would retrieve *TEACH* as well as *TEACHER, TEACHERS, TEACHING, TEACHES.*

Wild cards can also be helpful where there are variant spellings of a word, for example WOM?N would retrieve WOMAN or WOMEN.

Phrases

Many databases will automatically search two consecutive words as though they were joined by the Boolean operator AND, and will therefore return records in which both the words appear, but separated rather than as a phrase. Most tools allow you to search for a phrase by enclosing the words in quotation marks, although sometimes brackets are used, for example 'Secondary education' or (Secondary education).

Limiting your search

Many databases and search engines will allow you to limit your search to give you more control over your results. The most common ways that you can limit your search are:

- By *field*: you can tell a database to look for your keywords in a particular field of a document. You could choose to search for your keywords across all the text in a journal article, or you could choose just to search in the title fields. You will get vastly different results by experimenting this way.
- By *date:* you can usually tell the search tool to limit your search to a particular time period. This is very useful if you are looking for very current information.

Keeping a record of your searches

It is strongly recommended that you keep a record of all the searches you perform. This will help you to avoid duplicate effort and will also provide evidence of your research process. Most databases allow you to create a personal account and provide a facility for recording your search history. Check the help option of the particular database to find out how to do this; otherwise a writing pad and a pen will be sufficient.

Search summary

The flow chart in Figure 4.2 gives you a helpful pathway to follow when you are carrying out your research. Check that you have considered all the details necessary to complete each stage effectively.

Section 3: Evaluating information

This section aims to help you:

- know why it is important to evaluate the information you find;
- know what criteria you should use to evaluate the value of information.

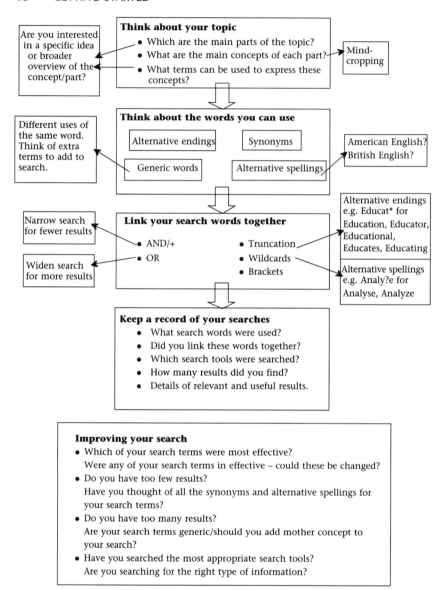

Figure 4.2: Search summary flow chart

When you are engaged in your research it is important that you are aware that not all printed and online information is appropriate for use in educational research. For a variety of reasons a significant proportion of the information you find, especially via the Internet, can be unreliable and unsubstantiated.

It is critical that you evaluate the information you find before you begin to use it within your own work. If you use information of a low standard you could base your arguments on incorrect information and jeopardize the integrity of your research.

Here are some questions to ask yourself when evaluating any information you find:

- Is the author writing from a biased viewpoint, resulting in an unbalanced review with limited perspective?
- Is the author qualified in his/her field? What else have they published? Are they accredited to a reliable institution or professional body?
- Who is the publisher of the information? Are they reputable?
- Is the information written to promote a commercial product or service?
- Is the information produced for entertainment, with no academic purpose intended?
- Has the information been through the Peer Review process? Some books and journal articles go through a process called 'peer review' in which panels of experts go through the information and comment on its quality. If peer-reviewed information is of a low quality the author will be asked to amend any mistakes before it is published, or the piece of work will be rejected altogether. Not all journal articles go through this process so not all journal articles are of the same quality.
- Is the writing style academic in tone or is it intended for a popular audience?
- Is the information supported by references to other work?

The following *ticklist evaluation tool* was devised by Kim McGowan (Learning Advisor, University of Cumbria); apply this to any websites that you intend to use in your research:

Trustworthy: Look at the domain name:
                       .com and **.co** are commercial sites
                       .org is a non-profit organization
                       .ac is a UK academic site and **.edu** is a US
                       educational site

	.gov is a UK government site
	.doh.gov.uk, .nhs.uk are health sites
Intention:	Who is it aimed at and why?
	Is 'Help' or 'about this site' available?
Currency:	When was it last updated and are links active?
Knowledge base:	How authoritative is the person or organization responsible and how credible is the information? Is there a contact email?
Level:	How detailed is the coverage; is it at the right level?
Information:	How accurate is the information? Use your subject knowledge or cross-reference details to check.
Support:	Is the information supported by references or citations?
Thoughts:	What do you feel about the overall presentation and content of the site?

Section 4: Using information appropriately

Once you have found the information you require for your research it is important that you go on to use it fairly and legally. Failure to do this may result in you breaking the law.

This section introduces you to the importance of:

- making copies of your sources legally (copyright law);
- ensuring that you do not steal the work of others (plagiarism);
- citing information sources you have referred to (referencing).

Copyright

If you wish to make a copy of a source of information it is your responsibility to ensure that you do not infringe copyright law. If you are making a single copy of information for your own use it is likely that this copy can be made under the 'fair dealing' guidelines. Many libraries and institutions own licences that allow additional copying under certain guidelines. More information about these licences is available from several sites listed in the further reading section of this chapter. Copyright applies to all types of information, including print and electronic information, sound recordings, sheet music, art and drama.

'Fair dealing' usually allows you to make the following copies for 'non-commercial' research or private study:

- one whole chapter or up to 5 per cent of a book (whichever is greater);
- up to 10 per cent of a short book or pamphlet (copying no more than 20 pages);
- one article from an issue of a journal or a conference proceeding;
- one poem or short story (of up to 10 pages) from an anthology;
- the report of one case from a law report;
- one separate illustration, diagram or photograph of up to A4 size from a book (more images than this may be copied if they are an integral part of a chapter you are using);
- one article from an issue of a newspaper.

Older works may no longer be protected within the copyright law; however, it is important to check that time has lapsed on all potential 'owners' of the copyright before assuming that you are legally able to copy this information freely.

Plagiarism

When using information it is important that you respect the 'moral rights' of the author(s) by ensuring that you always acknowledge the author of the information you use and refer to this information accurately in your work. Failure to state clearly the author of any information used in your work will result in plagiarism, whether you use direct quotes from the works you read, or whether you just paraphrase from the ideas or concepts. This applies to all types of information, whether published or unpublished.

To avoid plagiarism you should:

- Ensure that any quotations (direct copies of a piece of text) you use from other works are clearly enclosed within double quotation marks and are referenced accurately.

  It is best practice to avoid the use of too many quotations in your work.

  Large quotations should be avoided and separated from the rest of your text if used, for example indented.
- Paraphrased information (information from a source described in your own words) does not require the use of quotation marks but must still be referenced accurately to show that the ideas expressed are not your own.

- Any sources of information used in the construction of your work can be listed in a bibliography at the end of your work (see referencing) to show that these sources have influenced you.

Referencing

Referencing is the technique used to indicate which sources of information have been used in your work. It is essential that you reference your sources in full, giving accurate information in order to respect the moral rights of the authors whose work you refer to and to avoid plagiarism.

Many different referencing systems are used across the world. The most common systems include the 'Harvard' or 'author-date', the 'Vancouver' or 'numeric' and the 'MLA' and 'MHRA'. Whichever system you use you must ensure that you follow it consistently throughout your work, including all the necessary information.

You may find that if your work is for an accredited course, you will normally be instructed as to which system you will be required to follow by your tutor or institution.

There are two places in which you should include details of a reference in your work:

- A *citation* appears in the text of your work, wherever you use a quote or incorporate an idea you have gained from another source. This is often indicated by the use of a superscript number in the text or by the inclusion of the author's surname and date of publication (depending on which referencing system you are following).
- A *reference* provides the full details about the source you have cited in your text. It must give enough information so anyone else reading your work can track down the source item.

References should be listed at the end of your work in a reference list or bibliography, or you should insert them as footnotes on the page in your work where you refer to the source (depending again on which referencing system you are following).

A *reference list* is a list of references that should be inserted at the end of your work, and should only include the sources you have referred to and, therefore, have cited directly in your work.

A *bibliography* is an alphabetical list of references that should be inserted at the end of your work, which includes all the sources you used in the development of your work, not just those cited.

Examples of a full reference are given below, showing the same chapter in the same book referenced in two different systems:

- **Harvard**
  Fraser, J. and Hough, H. (2008) Information skills for classroom research, in S. Elton-Chalcraft, A. Hansen and S. Twistleton (eds.) (2008) *Doing Classroom Research: A Step-by-step Guide for Student Teachers*. Maidenhead: Open University Press.
- **Vancouver**
  Fraser, J. and Hough, H. Information skills for classroom research. In Elton-Chalcraft, S., Hansen, A., Twistleton, S., editors. *Doing Classroom Research: A Step-by-step Guide for Student Teachers*. Maidenhead: Open University Press; 2008.

Many referencing guides are available on the Internet. Some systems, like MHRA, have handbooks to follow, while other systems, like Harvard, have evolved over time, with many versions available. If you are ever unsure of which system to use you should ask the intended audience of your work which one they prefer (for example, a tutor or publisher) or look at other works in your field to see what the most commonly used system is.

Section 5: Recommended resources and suggested further reading

Always ask your library for help with any of the issues raised in this chapter; the library staff will be qualified to give you advice and support for all areas of your research.

Below is a small selection of online and print materials that you may find useful:

Research overview

Fink, A. (2005) *Conducting Research Literature Reviews: From the Internet to Paper*, 2nd edn. London: Sage Publications.

Queensland University of Technology (2006) *Online Information Literacy Tutorial* [Online]. Brisbane: Queensland University of Technology, www.pilot.library.qut.edu.au, accessed 5 July 2007.

University of Texas (2004) *TILT* [Online]. Texas: University of Texas, www.tilt.lib.utsystem.edu, accessed 5 July 2007.

Buzan, T. (2002) *How to Mind Map*. London: Thorsons.

Identifying the required information

Minneapolis Community & Technical College (2001) *Production of Knowledge* [Online]. Minneapolis: Minneapolis Community & Technical College, www.minneapolis.edu/library/tutorials/infolit/tablesversion/lessons/lesson1/production.htm, accessed 5 July 2007.

Searching skills

Intute (2006) *Intute – Virtual Training Suite* [Online]. Manchester: Intute, www.vts.intute.ac.uk, accessed 5 July 2007.
Open University Library (2001) *Safari* [Online]. Milton Keynes: Open University, www.open.ac.uk/safari/signpostframe.htm, accessed 5 July 2007.

Evaluating information

UNC College Libraries (2007) *Evaluating Information* [Online]. North Carolina: University of North Carolina, www.lib.unc.edu/instruct/evaluate/introduction, accessed 5 July 2007.
New Mexico State University Library (2006) *The Good, the Bad and the Ugly: or, Why It's a Good Idea to Evaluate Web Sources* [Online]. New Mexico: New Mexico State University, www.lib.nmsu.edu/instruction/eval.html, accessed 5 July 2007.

Copyright

Napier University (2008) *Copyright Tutorial* [Online]. Edinburgh: Napier University, www.napier.ac.uk/depts/ed/copyright/tutorial_3/index.html, accessed 5 July 2007.
Joint Information Systems Committee (1999) *Fair Dealing and 'Permitted Actions'* [Online]. Bristol, London: Joint Information Systems Committee, www.jisc.ac.uk/uploaded_documents/lis_Fair%20Dealing.pdf, accessed 5 July 2007.
Intellectual Property Office (2007) *Copyright – Basic Facts* [Online]. Newport: Intellectual Property Office, www.ipo.gov.uk/c-basicfacts.pdf, accessed 5 July 2007.

Referencing and Plagiarism

Pears, R. and Shields, G. (2005) *Cite them Right: The Essential Guide to Referencing and Plagiarism*. Newcastle upon Tyne: Pear Tree Books.
Napier University (2008) *Be Wise, Don't Plagiarise!* [Online]. Edinburgh:

Napier University, www.napier.ac.uk/depts/ed/copyright/tutorial_4/index.html, accessed 5 July 2007.

Pearson Prentice Hall (2007) *Understanding Plagiarism* [Online]. New Jersey: Pearson Education, www.wps.prenhall.com/hss_understand_plagiarism_1/0,6622,427064-,00.html, accessed 5 July 2007.

Glossary

alert services   most online journals and databases allow you to set up email alerts that will inform you of any new articles that match your search criteria. Also called current awareness tools.

Boolean operators   a system of code words that allow you to build complex searches, linking keywords together to narrow or broaden your search.

citation   a reference in your text to another author's work (listed in your reference list), often taking the form of the author's name you are referring to or the number of your corresponding reference.

conference proceedings   academic researchers regularly attend conferences where new ideas are presented; the proceedings are often published and can provide up-to-date information.

current awareness tools   see *alert services*.

full-text databases   tools that allow you to search collections of journals, providing the full text of your results electronically.

indexing databases   tools that allow you to search the bibliographical information of journals and provide you with all the information necessary for you to locate a journal article, but do not provide you with the full text.

keywords   words, phrases or synonyms that describe your research topic.

metasearch engine   an Internet search tool that searches across multiple web search engines.

mind-map   a diagramatic system that enables you to expand and refine your research ideas.

plagiarism   the use of another person's ideas or work without acknowledging them.

podcasts an Internet audio programme that users can subscribe to.

popular information information that is designed for general use, usually not requiring an academic knowledge of the subject to be understood.

primary information original research information, for example statistics, newspaper articles, conference proceedings, experiments, reports, patents, blogs and letters.

reference a piece of text that lists all the information a reader needs in order to identify and locate the source that you have cited in your work.

reference list a list of all the references for the sources you have cited in your work, and put in a list at the end of the main text.

secondary information written information that comments on or interprets primary information.

scholarly information high-quality academic information written by, and for, scholars in a particular field of study.

tertiary information summaries of a set of secondary information, such as encyclopaedia entries.

theses written reports of research projects undertaken for higher education qualifications such as masters or doctoral degrees.

truncation a search technique that allows you to search for variant endings of a word using a special symbol.

web search engine a tool that allows you to search for information that matches your keywords or phrases.

wild cards a search technique that can allow you to search for variant spellings of a word using a special symbol.

5 Ethical issues

Patricia Macpherson and Edward Tyson

Introduction

This chapter focuses on the ethical basis that must underpin all research and investigations in schools and/or settings.

This chapter aims to help you:

- appreciate that an ethical base must underpin all work that goes on in working with children and young people, including research;
- know about *ethical issues* connected with action research involving children and young people (see ethical checklist);
- understand the importance of *ethical conduct* before, during and after the data collection (see ethical research wheel).

Being an active researcher is a central feature of being a good teacher (see Chapters 1 and 2). You will have practised these skills already through, for example, lesson planning and review where some evaluation of your performance as a teacher and the children's responses and/or achievements has been completed. Your interpretation of this then informs future planning, teaching and learning in the classroom (see Chapters 4 and 8). If your analysis of this data is thorough then there is a great deal of validity to the judgements you have made and subsequent actions. If a surface approach has been taken to evaluation then there is obviously less validity and the actions taken are less likely to be successful in improving teaching and learning (see Chapters 6 and 10). There is also the chance that the real issues are overlooked and so poorer performance is reinforced.

Your approach to what might be more formal or designated research needs to be similarly responsible (Pollard 2002: 13) and honest so that your integrity as a researcher is not called into question.

What are ethics?

Ethics are not necessarily the same as morals but a notion of morality does inform our understanding of ethics. This understanding, though, is influenced by cultural positions and current acceptance of what is good practice. There are sound reference points to help here – BERA (2004) and UNICEF (1989) both provide guidance to help ensure that your research is ethically based. In addition, you may find that your own institution provides and expects you to conform to an identified structure for research and associated activity. As Dadds and Hart found out, it is not 'what' practitioners research but 'how' they research, as this is 'equally important to their motivations, their sense of identity within the research and their research outcomes' (Dadds and Hart 2001: 166).

In terms of being a teacher and undertaking research with children and young people, we have to consider also *meta-ethics*, which is the questioning of one's judgements. This means that while we expect teachers and intending teachers to be ethical in how they behave, we are also required to be ethical in how we think about issues and the results of investigations we make.

So how does this relate to you in your situation carrying out a piece of research or an investigation? First, you must meet the Professional Standards for Teachers (TDA 2007) where there are both explicit and implicit references to research-based activity. Good professional practice is about improving our teaching through reflection (see Chapters 2 and 8).

There is rich and diverse data available from the classroom that covers all aspects of school life and social life, personal and social; academic and cognitive; attainment and achievement; behaviour; organization and management; relationships with parent and carers; curriculum development and implementation; the impact of local, national and even international events.

What we need to bear in mind is that life in the classroom and school is essentially first and foremost an interpersonal relationship between:

- the teacher and pupils;
- the pupils themselves;
- teachers and other staff;
- staff, parents and carers;
- teachers, as researchers.

How situations are handled and how relationships are established are of prime importance. This is:

1 in recognition of the people we deal with when undertaking research in schools and classrooms. Basically, we enter other people's space and because of this we should always be mindful that we are a guest in the school;

2 in relation to the standards in professional value and practice, which apply to us all;

3 in acceptance of the explicit expectation within the wider research community for us to conduct research that is informed and underpinned by those ethics and values relevant to research with children and young people. These are:

- professional/ethical behaviour in designing, undertaking and interpreting research project;
- the notion of *informed consent*;
- meta-ethical considerations of the value and purpose of the research.

Using ethical guidelines

As we have just explained, ethical issues should be at the forefront of the research and not part of a checklist for your research project. Bearing this in mind, what do you need to do and how might you do it?

Obviously you will be following some ethical framework produced by your college, university or professional body. Such frameworks from BERA (2004), and so on contain the technical issues that you will need to explore before beginning your research. We have added another important issue to make 5 *Cs*, which are important issues for the researcher to consider:

1 *conduct* before, during and after the research has been undertaken;

2 *confidentiality* of responses and in terms of identifying participants within the research;

3 *consent* and permissions to undertake the research (possibly from a governing body or from your institution's ethical research committee);

4 *choosing* a methodology that is fit for the purpose;

5 *contextualizing*: addressing what is special and distinctive about your research question in relation to the children and young people who will be involved with that question.

It is essential that all these issues are considered when undertaking any research, no matter how small or short-lived it is, and no matter what its focus or purpose.

Ethical checklist

The following ethical factors need to be considered:

- Research question – is the question suitable/appropriate? Are the *participants* able to willingly take part in this research? Does the question address an ethically sound issue as well as meeting the requirements of your educational institution?
- Permissions – have the appropriate permissions been gained from the relevant educational establishment? Is further consent required from parents, carers or the children themselves (see letter on p. 67 at the end of this chapter)? Does this research need to go through an ethical committee?

  It should be noted that you cannot assume that you have obtained full permissions just because you may be working in the school or undertaking a teaching placement.
- Methodology – are the methods appropriate and suitable for the intended age range/ability of the participants?
- Access – do the participants have the necessary rights to opt in and out of the research? Do they know and understand the nature of the inquiry and will they have access to the findings?
- Safety – are there any requirements such as CRB clearances or child protection issues? Are you being left on your own with a child or are the children and young persons in groups or under the close supervision of staff from within the setting/school? Are you using ethical guidelines from your institution or from other recognized professional bodies like BERA?
- Data collection – has the data been gathered fairly without *bias*? Are the participants, the school or educational setting, the staff and their roles within the institution anonymous (as far as is practicable) (see Chapter 7)?
- Emotional conflict – are there any emotional issues that need addressing or disclosing and how might/have these affected the data?
- Data analysis – have you considered how you would validate the information for accuracy and relevance? How have you attempted to reduce your own bias and opinions (see Chapters 6 and 10)?
- Findings – have you been fair and honest in your judgements? Are the findings valid and are your recommendations drawn from the data or from your own beliefs and values?
- Publication – now the research has been completed what is its

intended audience? How are the findings going to be disclosed to the participants, and other bodies (see Chapters 11 and 12)?

Considerations of researching with children and young people

One of the prime considerations for carrying out any type of research with children and young people is how we view them within the research. Are they merely inert objects that we conduct research upon for the greater good? Are they subjects who have feelings that we need to consider, but who still have little influence in the design or the question of the study? Hopefully, they are participants in which a process of negotiation is undertaken, to set limits for the research, to illustrate the purpose and need for the research, to involve them more fully as stakeholders – as the research is for them and will give something back to them.

Obviously these views are affected by historical perspectives, social constructs of the times we live in and our own view on the role and nature of research. Scientific enquiry and the positivism paradigm of research have been blamed for the cold, clinical, uncaring approach to gathering data, but this is not necessarily the case. Good inquiry, whether quantitative or qualitative, should be considerate of its subjects, of their needs, feelings and rights. Strauss and Corbin propose that:

> Analysts as well as research participants, bring to the investigation biases, beliefs, and assumptions. This is not necessarily a negative trait; after all, persons are the products of their cultures, the times in which they live, their genders, their experiences, and their training. The important thing is to recognise when either our own or the respondents' biases, assumptions, or beliefs are intruding into the analysis.
> (1998: 97)

Action research projects usually refer to their subjects as participants. The key difference is that this implies that both parties, the researcher and the researched, are involved in the research – that they equally participate, that they have equal rights, consideration and emotions. They are free to take part in, to withdraw from, or even question the value of the research and/or research methodology (depending on their age and abilities).

This *participatory process* is not without complications. Often it is seen as being more complicated than scientific approaches as the researcher is closer to the research and, consequently, questions of validity and bias may be harder to establish. If one is 'in' the research it can be harder to establish the validity of the inquiry, as it is less likely for other researchers to repeat the process and come up with similar findings. Greater care is needed in the ethical considerations of bias. Always and regularly ask yourself the following questions:

1   Am I interpreting the research data objectively?
2   How do I know that I am?

Working 'in' the research is likely to engender feelings of significance and importance that may be less obvious to others outside of the research.

The notion of research 'done to' children and young people should be strongly avoided as it has little or no place in our society because there are many laws governing the rights of the child. Children are no longer seen as objects that we 'can do' research to without regard for their feelings and their right to participate in the research or not. Although research 'done with' could be considered to be ethical in our current social climate, it does not appropriately satisfy the wider considerations that children and young people have both the right to be aware of the research, but also have the right to be part of the research, to guide it, to be 'in' the research themselves. It still implies that an external influence (adult) is beyond the children's and young person's perceived understanding.

The notion of research working 'alongside' children or young people or action research, where the research is participatory, is preferable. This is because it is ethically stronger and it is an approach in which the children and young people may also be working 'as' researchers themselves. Action research is a very suitable means of enquiry in this area because it allows the researcher to be involved within the research: 'they recognise themselves as potential variables in the enquiry' (Bassey 1995: 13).

They know the purpose, the methodology and share in the findings. Such research is likely to prompt the participants to be more interested in the process and the findings, and these could be very significant as deeper involvement is likely to produce more data and lead to a deeper analysis and, therefore, greater findings. It can also help to reduce the possible bias (more voices identifying the same trends) as well as help to give the study more validity.

The participatory notion of research can, as outlined above, help to give increased benefits for bias and validity, as well as being ethically sound (see Chapter 7). It can also help the researcher in that it offers opportunities for a wider selection of research methods, as Alderson outlines (Farrell 2005: 30):

> Children as active participants take part willingly in research that has flexible methods: semi-structured interviews with scope for detailed personal accounts, exploring topics through focus groups, or drama, diaries, photos or videos, painting or maps created by the children. Increasingly, children are involved in planning, directing, conducting and/or reporting research projects.

Obviously it goes without saying that there are some limitations to the above methods as the age, ability and physical or emotional state of the child or young person will need to be considered carefully (see Chapter 9).

Whatever you chose to research, there will be some common themes to bear in mind as well as scenario-specific issues to consider. These relate back to the 5 Cs and it is likely that you will need to ensure that:

- careful and appropriate planning and conduct before, during and after your research is completed;
- anonymity for both children and staff taking part in your study is preserved;
- informed consent and participation is secured in advance;
- the methodology selected is appropriate not only in relation to the focus of your research but also with regard to the other 4 Cs.

Meta-ethical consideration

As we explained earlier in the chapter, meta-ethics is a questioning of one's own judgements, a questioning of the findings and claims we make.

Have we considered the nature of our inquiry? What are the reasons and implications behind the research question? Have we considered that there may be alternative approaches to both the question and the methodology? What role do the children and young people have in our research – are they objects, subjects or participants?

Murray and Lawrence (2000: 19) believe that ethical guidelines are more than just a set of rules; they see them as a 'mental template that translates the intellectual and moral obligations of practitioner-based research into steps for action in the enquiry setting'. Good research should begin with the ethical considerations. Ethics should pervade all aspects of the ethical research wheel (see Figure 5.1); too often it is 'bolted on' or simply a checklist for beginning a study. If we seek to put it

Ethics should pervade all aspects of the 'ethical research wheel at the heart of the inquiry then it can help to address several key problems/issues and can aid in the construction of a valid research proposal and methodology.

We have strongly encouraged the view that participatory research is preferable (for reasons cited earlier). We have also encouraged the notion that the researcher should be 'in' the research (this, too, was also explored earlier). However, problems and other ethical considerations can arise from adopting this particular research stance. Most practitioner researchers feel comfortable about exploring issues with children and young people (except where these touch upon sensitive issues) as they feel themselves to be in a different role, a position of power. That is to say that they are viewed as someone in authority, or someone that society has valued and given a significant role to, which the children or young people can identify with (that is class teacher or youth worker). Obviously one needs to be careful not to break or damage that position by careless or thoughtless acts or, equally important, through non-action

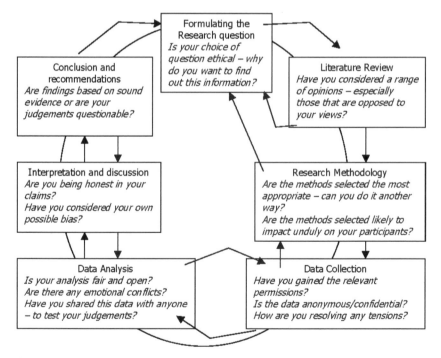

Figure 5.1 Ethical research wheel
Notes: Titles are the phases of research project writing. Italicized text denotes the ethical issues and considerations that should be reviewed before moving on to the next step on the wheel.

when the situation demands or requires action (for example children disclosing that they are being bullied or abused).

What happens when we step outside our comfort zone? If we are researching with children and young people we are less familiar with or where they see us less clearly as a person of power or significance, then the situation can be more demanding and emotionally more difficult. This is often the case when working with other adults in school or educational contexts. Have we the right to question others in authority over us? Can we explore the reasons and actions behind various decisions? By investigating the following scenario we can see how the researcher explores their emotional involvement with teachers and the head teacher in a primary school and their attempts at resolving these difficulties.

Case Study

The methodology chosen for the research was semi-structured interviews with the staff and head teacher; to ascertain their views on what they felt was leading to the continued lack of improvement in the children's mathematical ability and how they also felt that the situation could be improved. Permissions had also been obtained from the governing body of the school as the publication of the research was intended to inform for the school's action planning and curriculum development.

It soon became apparent that the head felt that she had to give her opinion as if it was the 'correct' and only rational view to address the situation. The head was not only using her influence but also her authority to influence the findings. This put a great deal of tension and emotion into the situation. These feelings increased prior to the publication of the data. As a result of analysing the data, only one person (the head) strongly proscribed changing the mathematic curriculum by adopting a scheme that has worked well in another local school. The majority of other participants felt that more modest changes were likely to improve the situation significantly.

The situation was only resolved by sharing my finding with my university tutor and a more mature member of staff when they made me realise that the best judges of the research findings would be the staff and governors of the school. By presenting the data in an open meeting then the results should speak for themselves. The interpretations and target-setting would be the result of informed discussion from all the stakeholders in the school.

Reflection on Case Study

What is clear from the case study is that the researcher had a good reason for their research and had identified the key people to interview in order to gain relevant and sufficient data. What they had forgotten was their own role and feelings in questioning the individual concerned and the tensions that that created both for the interviewee and the interviewer. The consideration here is not whether we should question people in significant roles (we should), but what feelings is that likely to engender in ourselves and will this impact on the validity of our research?

In situations where tensions exist it can be more difficult to analyse the data; either it is underanalysed or overanalysed, giving it greater or lesser importance. It, therefore, becomes biased, perhaps unknowingly so. What can be done?

- First, in the research methodology consider who will be conducting the research (that is doing the interviewing or making observations).
- Second, try to establish what relationship is between yourself and them (if you are conducting the research yourself).
- Third, consider if this is likely to engender tensions or implicate you.

It is sometimes very difficult to be truly objective depending on what you are investigating and the context in which you are carrying out the research. Greater objectivity can be achieved, for example, by someone else undertaking part of the research or the individual(s) involved writing or recording their responses and passing them onto you (see Chapter 9) concerning the benefits of collaborative research. Bassey (1995: 47) reminds us that 'involving people who are well known to the researcher, it seems to demand not only a strong ethic of respect for persons, but also democratic involvement on whom it impinges'. So, with all participants formal assent together with permissions from all stakeholders not only involves those participants in a fuller way but also gives them the licence to participate or not.

Research is the search for answers. Whether these answers result in new knowledge or lead to changes in practice, they should in some way inform our future decisions and actions. Action research as Kember (2000: 4) illustrates is: 'concerned with social practice; aimed towards improvement; a cyclical process; pursued by systematic enquiry; a reflective process; participative; determined by the practitioners'.

Because research is the search for answers, we should not be afraid of the findings we have reached (providing they are ethically sound and as free of bias as is reasonably possible). What we do need to do is share the findings with those involved, discuss them and where necessary amend them (particularly where the data is thin or the conclusions drawn are weak) before we publish them. Evans (2002: 136) expresses the opinion that the researcher should be 'telling it as it is', so that the data and analysis is not only recognized by the participants, but is understood and valued by them equally.

This may not be an easy approach, but research and action research is never easy (the reasons have been identified earlier in the chapter). As the researchers tend to be closer to the research and closer to the participants, there is likely to be a stronger emotional bond between the participants. This may be a cathartic experience, but the process is worth following through as emotional involvement is likely to engender a work of greater quality because the feelings we have are more likely to drive us towards deeper and insightful learning and findings.

Fullan (2003: 103) discusses the notion of vision and values needing to be connected to an additional motivating force, 'akin to the spiritual' and Senge et al. (2002: 551) explains clearly that 'Spirituality is not about religion. It is about the space, freedom and safety to bring our whole beings to work'. Fullan (2001) also frequently refers to our 'moral duty', as he argues that we should seek to change the existing values to promote a vision of educational institutions developing systems that have real power to 'make positive differences to the lives of all citizens' (2001: 11). You may wonder how your small-scale research can live up to this lofty aspiration but well-designed ethical research – even on a small scale – can help make a positive difference to all participants.

Research is often viewed as an individual pursuit or independent study. While this is true to a point, engagement with others, be it discussion or debate or asking a colleague to reflect on your data and findings, is likely to add depth to the validity and findings of your work. Such collaborative approaches are to be encouraged as participatory research brings the researcher closer to the research question. Collaborative discussions with other colleagues who are outside of the individual's research are more likely to review the work from a fresh standpoint and, hopefully, suggest changes or modifications that will enhance its quality (see Chapter 9).

While strictly not ethical considerations these discussions are likely to question the judgements and decisions of the researcher and, therefore, make the researcher reflect on these perspectives and, hopefully, encourage the researchers to re-question some of the initial assumptions and re-evaluate their findings. The biggest problem to such collaborative approaches is the lack of time between the researcher completing an almost finished draft (for review by colleagues) and the final submission for grading by his or her university or college tutor.

Conclusion

It is possible to justify anything within a research project but ethics demands justification for the right reasons. For example, you may not be able to gather data as planned because of something related to ethics, so you need to evaluate what the ethical issue is and redesign your methodology. If you approach research from a purely methodological stance then you might not see the ethical dimensions until the end. Good research means thinking about the ethics at the same time as the methodology. Another factor is recognizing who will get to read the research. If, for example, the governors of the school are interested in the scope of the project then you need to factor this in when deciding who the audience will be and, therefore, design your research project accordingly. So, as Evans (2002: 136) says, 'tell it as it is' but do make sure you tell it ethically, from the beginning to the very end.

Remember to address the following:

- professional/ethical behaviour in designing, undertaking and interpreting your research project (before, during and after);
- the notion of informed consent and/or assent;
- the consequences of not adopting a fully ethical approach.

Incorporating all these into your work should mean that you will have very few problems in making sure that your research is ethical in all respects and across all themes. As Dadds and Hart (2001: 166) say, it's not the 'what' it's the 'how' that matters.

Key texts

Lewis, A. and Lindsay, G. (2002) *Researching Children's Perspectives*. Buckingham: Open University Press.
The first two chapters (pp. 3–33) are a very useful guide into ethical issues and the UN convention on the rights of the child.

Farrell, A. (ed.) (2005) *Ethical Research with Children*. Buckingham: Open University Press.
As the title might suggest there are various chapters that may prove useful to the reader as they explore many aspects of ethical research with children. The third chapter (pp. 27–36), 'Designing ethical research with children' by Priscilla Alderson, is particularly useful for the reader as it provides useful insight into the reasoning for one's own research and encourages the reader to reflect on the nature of their enquiry and methodology.

Greig, A., Taylor, J. and MacKay, T. (2007) *Doing Research with Children*, 2nd edn. London: Sage Publications.
Chapter 9 (pp. 168–81), 'Ethics of doing research with children', provides a good overview of the ethical issues involved with children and young people, and is particularly good in exploring the aspects of 'informed consent' and 'gaining assess'. There is also a useful 'summary of good practice guidelines for research standards'.

Sample letter to parents/carers

Dear Parent/Carer

I am a student at the local university and, as part of my course and placement, I have to undertake a school/setting-based research project. I am working in Class/Year with Mr/Ms Teacher and I would like to study the following topic/theme/question ....

I am writing to ask permission to work with your child on this research project and to assure you that the project will have a firm ethical basis. The head teacher and my university supervisor have agreed my research question and methodology and will provide formal supervision of my work and conduct within the school.

The project will last ...... days/weeks and the results will be available at the school by ...... (for example the end of June).

If you are able to give permission please complete the proforma below and return it to school by ......

Thank you in advance. Please do not hesitate to contact me if you have any questions or require any further information.

Yours faithfully,

....
I give permission for my child .... to participate in the research project ....

I understand that I can withdraw my permission at any time (if I inform the researcher in writing)

Signed .... (parent/guardian)

Glossary

ethics   the moral rules and principals that are culturally acceptable to a society in order for it to function (see BERA and UNICEF guidelines); essentially the guiding principles in good research (see the 5 Cs).

ethical conduct, issues and frameworks   the ethics and values relevant to research with children and young people (see BERA guidelines for a framework or the 5 Cs), particularly; professional/ethical behaviour in designing, undertaking and interpreting research project, and the meta-ethical considerations of the value and purpose of the research.

five Cs (*conduct, confidentiality, consent, choosing, contextualizing*); essential requirements when undertaking any research.

informed consent   gaining the appropriate permissions from the relevant authorities (school or educational establishment, parents or carers and from the children themselves). It may also require approval of an ethical committee.

meta-ethics   questioning of one's own judgements, the requirement to be ethical in how we think about issues and the results of investigations that we make.

participants   the subjects (or stakeholders) taking part in an action research project – see *participatory research*.

participatory process/research   where the researcher and the researched (participants) are involved equally in the research with rights, considerations and involvement (stakeholders).

References

Bassey, M. (1995) *Creating Education Through Research*. Newark/Edinburgh: Kirklington Moor Press and British Educational Research Association (BERA).

BERA (2004) *Revised Ethical Guidelines for Educational Research (2004)*, BERA [Online], www.bera.ac.uk/publications/pdfs/ETHICA1.PDF, accessed 12 July 2007.

Dadds, M. and Hart, S. (2001) *Doing Practitioner Research Differently*. London: Routledge Falmer.

Evans, L. (2002) *Reflective Practice in Educational Research*. London: Continuum.

Farrell, A. (ed.) (2005) *Ethical Research with Children*. Buckingham: Open University Press.

Fullan, M. (2001) *Change Forces: The Sequel*. London: Falmer Press.

Fullan, M. (2003) *Change Forces: With a Vengeance*. London: Routledge Falmer.

Kember, D. (2000) *Action Learning and Action Research*. London: Kogan Page.

Murray, L. and Lawrence, B. (2000) *Practitioner-based Enquiry*. London: Falmer Press.

Pollard, A. (2002) *Reflective Teaching: Effective and Evidence-informed Professional Practice*. London: Continuum.

Senge, P. *et al.* (2002) *The Dance of Change*. London: Nicholas Brealey.

Strauss, A. and Corbin, J. (1998) *Basics of Qualitative Research*, 2nd edn. London: Sage Publications.

Training and Development Agency (TDA) (2007) *Professional Standards for Teachers*, www.tda.gov.uk/teachers/professionalstandards/standards/attributes/relationships/qts.aspx?keywords=professional+standards, accessed 19 November 2007.

UNICEF (1989) *Convention on the Rights of the Child*, UNICEF [Online], www.ohchr.org/english/law/pdf/crc.pdf, accessed 12 July 2007.

Acronyms

BERA	British Educational Research Association
UNICEF	United Nation's International Children's Emergency Fund
TDA	Teacher Development Agency
CRB	Criminal Records Bureau

6   Reliability and validity

Martyn Lawson and Carey Philpott

The aim of this chapter is to:

- consider *reliability* and *validity* (definitions in glossary) of *quantitative* and *qualitative* (definitions in glossary) research data;
- alert you to some of the key potential pitfalls and offer some help in avoiding these;
- help you to be realistic about the claims you can make from your research.

Many of the 'scrutineers' of reliability and validity in your research will be people other than you. At first they might be tutors marking assignments, then they might be peer reviewers for conferences and journals (see Chapters 11 and 12). Although it might be inescapable that you have to convince someone else of the validity and reliability of your research in order to pass the module or get published, it is a mistake to focus on these others exclusively. If you are carrying out research designed to improve your own practice and benefit the learning of your pupils, it is more important that *you* are convinced of the validity and reliability of what you have done (see Chapter 5 concerning ethical issues). There is little point in managing to convince others that your data is valid and reliable if you know that problems you have disguised mean that the research was of no real value to you in understanding or improving what you do.

Reliability and validity quantitative research

The validity of quantitative research is usually concerned with two basic questions. First, is the sample you are examining a valid sample – that is does the sample represent a reasonable cross-section of the whole population? For example, if you are looking at the performance of pupils in a class, are the pupils typical of the pupils in the school, and are the pupils in the school typical of the school population as a whole?

For any researcher, this aspect of validity has an impact on the way that the research is conceived and constructed. Your choice of what to research and where needs to be thought through carefully and you need to be prepared to justify the decisions you make and relate them to your aims (see Chapter 7). For the classroom practitioner engaging in small-scale classroom research this may appear to present an insurmountable problem. Yet it need not, as long as you have thought through the implications of conducting research within your own school and classroom context. One common way of increasing the validity of your sample is to use random sampling. In this case the population to be studied is chosen at random from the population as a whole, so the likelihood of the sample being non-representative is reduced. In classroom- or school-based research this may not always be possible, but other techniques may help to ensure that the sample is as representative as it can be. Rather than randomly selecting subjects, you could establish some selection criteria and then ensure that a fair balance of subjects was chosen that covers those criteria. This is known as stratified sampling. For example, if you were looking to study the effects of a particular teaching method on the performance of a class at GCSE, you could ensure that your sample included pupils from all ability levels by using a baseline assessment as part of your selection criteria. Other criteria may be selected to ensure that the sample population is not biased in a particular way, so it might be appropriate to ensure that the sample is gender-balanced, or has an ethnicity balance that is in line with the school context. As a researcher it is part of your job to ensure that you select your sample carefully. There are other methods of selecting samples from the population and a good statistics text will describe them in more detail.

Second, validity is concerned to establish that the particular type of measurement you use is closely related to what you are measuring. A valid means of measurement is one that is consistent with what it thinks it is measuring. As a trivial example, it would not be valid to try and measure a pupil's practical performance in the long jump by asking them to write an essay about it! While this aspect of validity may appear less of a problem to the small-scale researcher, it still requires that you think carefully and plan ahead to ensure that the way you are researching is appropriate for what you are studying. Often researchers use things like questionnaires and interviews as a means of generating data. There is nothing wrong with these instruments in themselves, but their use must be appropriate to the questions you are studying. The examination of 'data-gathering methods' in Chapter 7 has much more to say about the ways in which you can collect your evidence.

Essentially, reliability is a subset of validity. If the techniques you use to collect your data are unreliable, then they will produce data that are by their very nature invalid. Reliability of data collection relates to the consistency of the measurement. The central question is whether the instrument of measurement you have used in your study is likely to produce the same results tomorrow as it did today (all other things being equal). If it is, then the measure is reliable. If not, then the unreliability of your chosen means of measurement could call into question your results.

For the researcher following a quantitative approach, there are some specific measures that can be used to determine the validity and reliability of the measurement undertaken in the study. For researchers following a qualitative approach, validity and reliability have to be determined in a different way, which is discussed in the next section. There are many excellent books about quantitative measures and methods that can be used in research; at the end of the chapter there is a sample reading list that provides some of these.

This part of the chapter is not going to concentrate on statistics; however, it is important to understand some basic concepts so that you can avoid some of the pitfalls that quantitative research could hold.

First, when researchers refer to the population, they are talking about the whole population of the group under study. So, if we were interested in looking at some aspect of Year 7 pupils, the population would consist of all the Year 7 pupils in the country. Very few research projects can hope to access data of this magnitude, so in small-scale research we are more frequently concerned with a sample of the population. Hence, a sample is a small subset of the whole population. As suggested above, selecting your sample carefully is very important in trying to achieve validity for your research.

Second, it is important to realize that quantitative data can be used for different purposes and deciding on the most appropriate type of data to collect is vital to ensure that your analysis is both valid and reliable. If you try to use an inappropriate type of data in your quantitative analysis, you will produce results that are at best meaningless, but at worst misleading.

Case Study 1

> 1 A teacher carried out some research into classroom performance of
>   her pupils. She collected raw scores from a series of homework
>   tasks, then converted them into percentages.

2 The conversion of the scores into percentages allowed the teacher to undertake a comparison of pupil performance in all the tasks, so each score could be realistically compared with the others. Then she aggregated all the percentage scores for each pupil and converted them to produce an average score for each gender. From this she concluded that the girls in her class were performing at a higher level than the boys.

Reflection on Case Study 1

The first stage was appropriately conducted. Unfortunately, the second stage was a step too far! The aggregation and averaging makes this analysis suspect and potentially invalid because in the averaging of the percentages, one low score or one low-performing pupil could bring the whole average for the boys in the class down. So the effect of one pupil in the class could be changing the overall picture considerably. In this case, drawing conclusions about the whole pupil cohort in a class should be carefully considered and the data analysed appropriately. A much more valid comparison of cross-gender performance in this instance could be achieved by looking at performance for each task and using the raw data. In small-scale research there is seldom so much data that it needs to be overprocessed with aggregation and averaging. The raw data is much more illuminating.

Lastly, it is important to understand the concept of a normal distribution because it is central to the way in which validity and reliability are ensured in quantitative research. The concept is straightforward and an example, as shown in Figure 6.1, explains the idea.

The graph in the figure represents the scores of a group of students in a test. The x axis represents the score in the test, the y axis represents the number of students (the higher up the axis, the greater the number). On the x axis, the number 60 represents the arithmetic mean mark. The height of each bar of the graph represents the number of students who scored a particular score in the test. As we can see, most students scored 60. The other numbers represent scores less than or greater than the mean score. By looking at the graph, we can see that at the extremes there are relatively few scores in these areas. If you want to use a normal distribution curve or graph in your analysis of data, we would suggest that you consult a good textbook on statistics or quantitative research methods.

This kind of curve works in many circumstances. We could use a curve like this to model the height of students in a class. Probably, very few students would be really small or really tall. Most students would be

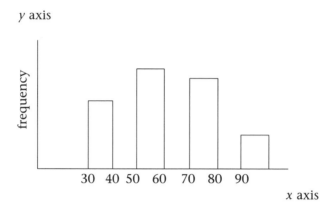

y axis

frequency

30 40 50 60 70 80 90

x axis

Figure 6.1 Scores of a group of students in a test

around the average height. This effect is known as 'central tendency'. We do need to be cautious here. If we consider the heights of children in Year 6 in one school, it would not be a particularly accurate indicator of heights of children in general. One very tall child could affect the overall distribution of heights in the class in a significant way. However, if the sample was based on the whole country, the effect of major differences in height of a small part of the population would be very small and so the overall data would be much more valid and reliable. Thus, the size of your sample has a direct bearing on the accuracy of fit to this normal distribution – the larger the sample, the more it will comply with the normal distribution and the more valid and reliable the data will be.

There are some excellent examples of the use of normal distribution data in large-scale longitudinal studies such as those carried out by the Curriculum, Evaluation and Management Centre at Durham University. You may have met some of these studies in school in things like Pips, InCas, Midyis, Yellis, Alis. These studies incorporate large samples of children and they have been collecting data for many years, so they can be confident in the validity and reliability of the data that they collect and the predictive nature of the individual scores that a child obtains in the testing instrument.

Knowledge of the normal distribution and the central tendency is useful to you as a researcher. Due to the small size of your data set, it is unlikely that your data will conform precisely to a normal distribution. However, if your data indicate large differences from an expected distribution, this could be indicative of a phenomenon worth exploring in detail. In this case, your data are showing where it might be useful to research in greater depth to find out why your analysis varies from the expected distribution.

In classroom research, you are likely to gather relatively small amounts of data, so there is a potential problem about generalizing from your research. With a small-scale survey, the findings of your classroom research cannot be used on their own to make general claims about some element of education. Claims like this would be invalid. However, your findings may prove useful in supporting an already existing body of research, or they may be useful to illustrate something that is specific to a particular school or setting. Your research is valuable, but be very careful about the claims you make for it.

The main message in this part of the chapter is to keep it simple. If you are collecting quantitative data in your research, plan well in advance what data you require and how you are intending to use it. Resist the temptation to overanalyse and process your data. As we have seen in some of the examples above, inappropriate use of data can render your research invalid and unreliable.

Reliability and validity in qualitative research

In much qualitative research you may be less concerned whether the sample you generate data from is representative of a larger population. This might be because you are doing an in-depth study of a smaller group or because, within practitioner research, you are less concerned with generalizing to all other pupils as long as your claims are valid for your pupils. In this context, validity is about whether the data you have generated is likely to show what you think it does, or could something else account for it or distort it in some way. Once again, reliability is linked to this idea: would you get the same data if you generated it at a different time?

This section looks at some of the most popular methods of generating qualitative data used by education students and considers the challenges for reliability and validity of each (see also Chapter 7). All methods of qualitative data generation have drawbacks. The important thing is to be aware of them, how you are going to reduce them and how you are going to take account of them in your interpretation of the data.

Questionnaires

Questionnaires are popular with education students because they seem easy to use and 'the sort of thing that researchers do'. However, questionnaires present many validity issues. It is worth considering whether you need to use questionnaires if you are adopting a qualitative approach. One of the attractions of questionnaires is the large number of responses in a standard form you can get apparently easily. This might be valuable when using quantitative methods but is less meaningful when using qualitative methods.

One validity consideration with questionnaires is that you only get the answers to the questions you ask. The questions you choose to use might suggest that you already know what the key issues are. Writing a questionnaire can shut out a range of possible factors that might be relevant.

The more 'closed' questions are, the more this is an issue. One possibility is constructing questionnaires with more 'open' questions that allow a range of responses, including unexpected ones (see Chapter 7). Another possibility is to use interviews rather than questionnaires. Or you can combine both by using a number of 'open' interviews and then using these to construct more informed questionnaires.

Another validity problem for questionnaires is that respondents misunderstand the questions. A solution is to pilot the questionnaires. Piloting means trying them out with a small group who can feedback on how well they understood the questions. The more similar this group is to the people you will use the questionnaire with, the better.

Asking people to complete questionnaires while you wait also raises validity considerations. It might be that respondents do not have particularly strong or clear views about the questions you ask but they write something to get it finished. If they are expected to give the completed questionnaire to you, they might be reluctant to give certain kinds of answers.

These are difficult issues to avoid completely. However, try to avoid administering questionnaires in ways that make the problems worse. Avoid giving people too short a time to complete questionnaires that might lead to ill-considered answers. Avoid doing them when people can go as soon as they have finished. Make it clear that 'I don't know' is an acceptable response. It is better to know that people are unclear about what they think than it is to have them invent an opinion or adopt a formulaic or expected response just to finish the questionnaire. If questionnaires are completed while you are there, collect them so that you cannot see the responses as they are handed in.

Allowing people to take questionnaires away presents additional validity considerations. 'Take away' questionnaires typically have a low number of returns. This raises questions about whether the returns you have represent the whole group. People who have strong views are often more likely to respond. Those who have no strong views are likely to be overrepresented among the non-respondents.

Case Study 2

A student surveyed a Year 5 class of 30 about their views on sports day and found that, in 12 returns, six were extremely positive about it and six extremely negative. Would it be valid to conclude that attitudes in the class were polarized?

Interviews

Interviews can be divided into three types: structured, semi-structured and unstructured. Structured interviews are like questionnaires that are completed orally. This approach is often used to promote consistency in large-scale (often quantitative) surveys and is less relevant in small-scale research. However, it might be an approach that you would consider if surveying very young children. The validity issues for structured interviews are very similar to some of those considered previously for questionnaires. They have the advantage over questionnaires of allowing for clarification of questions but they also have similar validity challenges to other kinds of interviews.

Semi-structured interviews use a set of standard questions but allow you to add questions in response to answers that have been given. In terms of validity, these have the advantage of not assuming that you know all the right questions to ask before you start.

Unstructured interviews can be open-ended. In validity terms, they have the advantage over questionnaires in that they allow respondents to talk about the issues that are important to them rather than the ones you thought were important. Another validity advantage of unstructured interviews is that they are more like ordinary conversations. This can mean that people give more 'natural' responses in them than they might do in the more unfamiliar and formal situation of the questionnaire or the structured interview. This kind of approach means that you can consider a range of naturally occurring conversations as data and as a useful indication of what people think. We need to be careful, in validity terms, about the idea of 'natural' responses, hence the inverted commas. We return to this below.

Perhaps the main validity issue for interviews is the influence that you as the interviewer will have on the interviewee (see Chapter 5). The relationships you have with respondents (for example teacher–pupil, mentor–trainee) might influence the answers you get. In general, people may just be reluctant to reveal certain kinds of things to anyone face to face and be more willing to share them in the relative anonymity of a questionnaire.

There are no easy solutions to these challenges. Because of the nature of the research you are doing, you will nearly always have a relationship with those you interview that can influence their responses. Part of the solution lies in the wider nature of the relationships you have with interviewees and what they understand about your research. What signs have you given that you welcome honest responses no matter how unpalatable? Do they understand that you are carrying out an enquiry designed to help them and not an inquisition?

Some education student researchers have found that getting pupils to talk to one another in groups about the issues that they are researching can be helpful. This has allowed the researcher to be less obtrusive. However, we also need to be aware of the ways in which these groups might be influenced by peer pressure.

'Real world' data

So far we have considered validity issues for qualitative data generated specifically for your research. You can also use qualitative data that already exists. Alternatively, you could use observations to see what people do or say in contexts other than the research survey.

Using already existing documents such as pupils' writing, school policies or government documents, might help overcome some of the validity problems discussed above that relate to specially generated data. However, you still need to take account of the audience and purpose for which these documents were written. A departmental policy document on homework that will be included in information given to parents might not straightforwardly represent the views on homework of school staff or even the person who wrote it. It will represent the particular articulation of it that was considered appropriate for that audience and that purpose.

Watching what people do in action can also help to reduce the types of validity challenges that you might experience when generating data specially. Again, we need to acknowledge that what people say or do in a particular context is part of that context and that in another context they might speak or act differently. This was the reason for our earlier caution about 'natural answers'. This means that observations are most valid when they are of the context that you are researching and when you do not assume that opinions expressed or actions carried out in one context represent views or behaviour in a general way. Observations can be useful for overcoming the difference that can exist between what people say and what they do in practice. This gap is not necessarily caused by conscious misrepresentation. People can be mistaken about what they actually do when they report their behaviour.

Case Study 3

A group of Year 7 pupils claimed in a questionnaire that they did no reading outside of school. When observed, they read TV guides, signs, instructions, websites, video games but did not think of this as reading.

Reliability

In the types of examples we have discussed above, reliability and validity merge because validity has been closely tied to the way that the context affects the nature of the data you generate. A way of thinking about reliability as a separate issue from validity is to ask, would you get the same response from the same respondents, using the same method at a different time?

Triangulation

One way of addressing issues of validity is triangulation. In simple terms this means using more than one source of data so that you can check your interpretation of one against the other.

Conclusion

The considerations of this chapter might make you feel gloomy about the prospect of being able to base any claim on the data you have. However, this would be a mistaken conclusion. You cannot remove all validity and reliability challenges completely. The trick is to show that you are aware of them, take steps to minimize them and take account of them in your interpretations and knowledge claims. Within the world-view of much qualitative research, it is misguided to try to arrive at a point at which we think we can claim that our data is objectively true and undistorted by the methods of generation. This is not actually possible. It is better to openly acknowledge reliability and validity problems and the ways in which they limit what we can claim to know on the basis of our research. One final way of thinking of validity and reliability relates to the practices of action research. If you are researching to improve the outcome of your practice and the changes you make to practice result in the improved outcomes you want, you can make a fair claim that the data on which you based your changes was valid (that is meant what you thought it meant).

Glossary

qualitative research   research that is not based on precise measurement of observed phenomena.
quantitative research   research that uses precise and mathematically or statistically provable techniques for measuring observed phenomena.

reliability   the extent to which repeated use of a measurement under the same conditions produces the same results.

validity   the success of a method of measurement in measuring exactly what it claims to measure.

Further reading

Bryman, A. (2004) *Social Research Methods*. Oxford: Oxford University Press.
Denscombe, M. (2004) *The Good Research Guide for Small-scale Social Research Projects*. Maidenhead: Open University Press.
Hinton, P.R. (2004) *Statistics Explained*, 2nd edn. Hove: Routledge Falmer.
Huff, D. (1973) *How to Lie with Statistics*. London: Penguin.
Knight, P.T. (2002) *Small-scale Research*. London: Sage Publications.
Mason, J. (2002) *Qualitative Researching*. London: Sage Publications.
McMillan, J. H. and Schumaker, S. (2006) *Research in Education*, 6th edn. Boston: Pearson Education Inc.

Oppenheim, A.N. (1966) *Questionnaire Design and Attitude Measurement.* Aldershot: Gower.

Ritchie, J. and Lewis, J. (2003) *Qualitative Research Practice.* London: Sage Publications.

Taber, K.S. (2007) *Classroom-based Research and Evidence-based Practice.* London: Sage Publications.

Willis, J.W. (2007) *Foundations of Qualitative Research.* London: Sage Publications.

Useful website

www.cemcentre.org

Part III Research strategies

7 Doing research in the classroom

Deborah Roberts and Adrian Copping

Objectives

This chapter aims to develop your understanding of:

- the importance of planning your research project carefully at the outset;
- key elements in designing a successful research project;
- posing appropriate research question(s);
- research methods at your disposal.

For the new researcher with many competing demands on his or her time, beginning a research project can be a daunting step. As a student in Initial Teacher Education, you are already expected to demonstrate such a diverse range of skills, knowledge and abilities, and those associated with research are yet another set to learn. This chapter sets out some key elements in designing a research project and introduces you to some of the main research methods at your disposal. It is introductory in nature aiming to familiarize you with the parameters of a research project, and options open to you. Once you feel more comfortable within these parameters, you will be ready to go on to further reading referenced throughout and at the end of the chapter.

Finding a research focus

Perhaps one of the most important steps in designing your research project will be to select an appropriate area upon which to focus your research and then, critically, pose a relevant question or questions. Authors, for example Edwards and Talbot (1999), will attest to the fact that it is important to choose an area that is of personal interest to you. If you are to commit time and effort to a project, then the more interesting this project is to you, then the easier it will be to sustain. In selecting an area for your research project you might want to consider issues or topics that intrigue or interest you, or perhaps those that have proved challenging – all may provide rich areas for research. Although not an exhaustive list, you might like to review the options on the following page listed under '*What am I interested in?*'.

Case Study 1

'What am I interested in?'
Paula, a student with a particular interest in special educational needs, chose as her area of investigation Asperger's Syndrome and Autism in mainstream school settings.

'Within this area of interest, what do I want to find out about?'
Within this area of interest, she particularly wanted to find out what constituted good inclusive practice for children with Asperger's Syndrome.

'Is the scale of this project manageable, within the time and resources that I have available?'
Paula succeeded in selecting a manageable focus within her area of interest, formulating the following question: 'What facilitates inclusion for one child with Asperger's Syndrome in a mainstream school?' Note here, the more manageable focus of one child in one setting. She then formulated a small number of sub-questions that helped direct her research project:
'What are the focus child's views of his schooling?'
'What facilitates inclusion for the focus child according to the class teacher?'
'What facilitates inclusion for the focus child according to the SEN co-ordinator?'

'Will I have access to willing research respondents within the time-scale of my project? Who are these respondents likely to be?'
This student was fortunate in having existing good contacts with a school and child, meaning that access was unlikely to be an issue. However, formal approval was still required from the head teacher, all participants and the parents of the focus child.

> *'Which method will help me to answer my research question(s)?*
> Paula chose to use semi-structured interviews to answer her questions. In contrast to questionnaires, which she also considered, she felt an interview situation with participants with whom she was already had some rapport would yield more detailed information. Further, semi-structured interviews allowed her to ask comparable questions of all her participants, while allowing the flexibility to probe for further detail.

Reflection on Case Study 1

Ask yourself *'What am I interested in?'*

- *an area of specialist knowledge* that I may have studied in some depth, for example a subject strength such as science, ICT or history;
- *an area of interest from my classroom experience,* for example technologies such as interactive whiteboards, or particular groups such as traveller children;
- *a challenging area for me or others,* for example working with and managing teaching assistants;
- *an area currently topical within education:* while these will change over time you will remember headlines about, for example, boys under achievement and bullying in schools.

Once you have selected an area of interest, your next step must be to focus in and pose a relevant question or questions. Focusing in on a specific question(s) is particularly important, as your whole research project will flow from this question(s). Cohen and Manion similarly describe a process of delimiting the topic to allow a 'more potent analysis' (1994: 47).

Ask yourself *'Within this area of interest, what do I want to find out about?'*

It might help to consider your research as an intellectual puzzle, and Mason (2002: 18) suggests a number of such puzzles. While a variation on, or combination of these puzzles may be more relevant to your project, each is described separately for the purposes of discussion.

- *Developmental puzzles* ask how and why did x or y develop? An example might be, how does a child's understanding of sentence structure develop?

- *Mechanical puzzles* ask how does x or y work? You might, for example, be interested in investigating how behaviour management works in your school.
- *Comparative puzzles* ask what can be learnt from comparing x and y? You might wish to conduct an international comparison of school curricula, or compare the likes and dislikes of girls and boys.
- *Causal/predictive puzzles* ask what influence x has on why or what causes x or y? Why do some children refuse to come to school or why do some children dislike certain school subjects?

Of course, a particular area of interest, for example excluded pupils, could be addressed by any of the above puzzles; we might, for example, compare a number of excluded children to see what they have in common (a comparative puzzle) or we could puzzle over why these children have been excluded (a causal puzzle); further, we could investigate how school exclusion works (a mechanistic puzzle). Considering your area of interest with reference to Mason's puzzles may be another way to help you focus your area of interest and define your research questions.

At this stage many students have quite ambitious ideas for their research project, and so it is also important to assess the manageability of your project, given all the other demands on your time such as placements, taught courses and other assignments.

Ask yourself: *'Is the scale of this project manageable, within the time and resources that I have available?'*

Supportive discussion with your supervisor should help you with this process of successive focusing, and identification of clear, focused and manageable research question(s). However, it would be wise at this early point to ensure, before too much time is committed to the project, that you will have access to willing research respondents. Access to teachers, classrooms and children is likely to be through head teachers. While it is important to have the support of your participants, key personnel such as head teachers act as 'gatekeepers' and are critical for gaining official access. Bryman (2001) suggests that access is facilitated by providing a clear explanation of the aims and method of your project. It would also be wise to cover ethical issues such as the intended outcomes of the project and anonymity of participants (for further consideration of ethical issues, see Chapter 4).

Ask yourself: *'Will I have access to willing research respondents within the time-scale of my project? Who are these respondents likely to be? Who might I need to contact for official access?'*

Preparation and design

Having successfully identified a focus, questions for your study and considered the practicalities of access to potential respondents, you are in a strong position to move forward with your overall research design.

Denscombe (2002) provides a most useful 10-point guide – a step-by-step guide of points to consider in designing a good research project. What we attempt to do here in Table 7.1 is to present Denscombe's 10 points with specific reference to the small-scale classroom-based research project. At the design stage, we suggest that you read through this table, reflecting upon each ground rule in turn, as an aid to planning your research project.

Methods of data-gathering

Reading Denscombe's ground rules and the associated questions will have encouraged you to reflect on a range of pertinent issues. One critical step to take is to select a research method or methods that will allow you to answer your questions. You will find many whole textbooks devoted to one research method or another such as textbooks on interviewing or questionnaire design. As an emerging small-scale researcher, it can be hard to know where to start. We will attempt to give you an overview of some of the main methods at your disposal, with a brief consideration of some of their strengths and weaknesses. Table 7.2 gives an 'at-a-glance' summary of some of the major advantages and disadvantages associated with each method; see also Chapter 6 concerning validity and reliability. You *will* also need to refer to other more detailed methodological textbooks for your chosen methods, and recommended reading is included at the end of this chapter. As you read through these methods:

Ask yourself: *'Which method will help me to answer my research question(s)?*

Interviews

Typically, interviews represent a one-to-one discussion with an interviewer, sometimes leading by asking questions to which the interviewee

Table 7.1: Ground rules for good research

Denscombe's Criterion	Denscombe's Ground Rule	Application to your small-scale project
1. Purpose	Research should have clearly stated aims	• Define your area of interest (*e.g. Special Educational Needs and Inclusion, and Asperger's Syndrome and Autism in mainstream school settings*). • Pose clear question(s) which indicate the focus of your research.
2. Relevance	Research should relate to existing knowledge and needs	• Explain why your research is important. • From reviewing the literature, what do you know already? • How does the literature relate to your research questions?
3. Resources	Research should recognize the constraints that time, money and opportunity impose	You are working to a deadline (a submission date) so it is critical that your project is focused and manageable. • Will you have access to willing research respondents? • Plan out your time to review the literature, plan your project, collect your data, analyse your data and write up your project. • How does this plan fit with other constraints on your time?
4. Originality	Research should contribute something new to knowledge	As a beginning researcher it may be difficult to have a thorough knowledge of an area, but reviewing existing literature and consulting your tutor will help here. • Can you identify an aspect of your research that is original? Perhaps you are investigating a topic in a different way, providing up-to-date data on a topic, or filling a gap in existing knowledge.
5. Accuracy	Research should produce valid data using reliable methods	• Are your methods valid (i.e. will they allow you to gain an accurate view of your research focus)? • Are your methods reliable (i.e. will they generate data that is consistent? Would your respondents give similar responses at a different time or in a different place)? *See also Chapter 5*

6. Accountability	Research should include an explicit account of its methodology	• Is there a good match between the question(s) you have posed and the methods you have chosen? • Justify why you have chosen your methods (*e.g. why was a semi-structured interview the most appropriate research method?*). • Explain why other methods are less appropriate (*e.g. why was a self-completion questionnaire not used?*).
7. Generalizations	Research should produce findings from which generalizations can be made	Your small-scale research is unlikely to be generalizable in the sense that it can be used to predict future events. However, tentative suggestions can be made that others might want to consider in the context of their own classrooms. In this way, the audience takes a decision on the generalizability of your findings. • What tentative claims can you make about your findings or research process that might be of interest to others?
8. Objectivity	Researchers need to be open-minded and self-reflective	Your view of objectivity will vary with the paradigm you associate yourself/your research with (see Chapter 1). However, within educational/social research you should consider and record: • the beliefs and values that you bring to your research, and a recognition that there will be competing beliefs and values • the effect that these beliefs/values will have on the research question, method, analysis and outcomes.
9. Ethics	Researchers need to recognize the rights and interests of participants	• Will your research harm or disadvantage your participants in any way? • Do your participants understand the nature of their involvement in your project (e.g. subject matter, time required)? • Are participants clear about the anonymity of data they provide? *See also Chapter 4*
10. Proof	Researchers need to be cautious about claims based on their findings	• Make tentative claims that recognize the limitations of your project. • Ensure that your findings are closely linked to your evidence. • Show that you have considered alternative interpretations.

Source: Ground rules reproduced from *Ground Rules for Good Research* (Denscombe 2002) with the kind permission of the Open University Press.

Table 7.2:

Method	Advantages	Limitations
Interview	• Can generate detailed and in-depth data • Where there is a trusting relationship between the interviewer and interviewee, can allow personal or sensitive issues to be explored	• Time-consuming for participants and researchers • Transcription is time-consuming for researchers • Analysis can be complex
Questionnaire	• Time efficient to administer • Analysis likely to be more straightforward • A good response rate from face-to-face questionnaires	• Data may lack depth and detail • Inability to follow up areas of interest, or question responses that are unclear • Requires very careful wording of questions to avoid misunderstanding/generate data required • Lower response rate from questionnaires completed independently
Focus groups	• Time efficient to administer • Can generate detailed and in-depth data	• Analysis can be complex • Effective facilitation skills may be required • Less suitable where personal matters are to be addressed • Transcription is time-consuming for researchers

| Observation | • Useful for investigating non-verbal behaviours
• Provides first-hand evidence of behaviour (as opposed to reported behaviour as in questionnaires/interviews) | • Biases might affect observations
• People rarely act the same when they know they are being observed
• May not provide explanations for observed behaviours and, therefore, may need to be combined with other methods |
| Discourse analysis | • Creates data about the language used in a given situation
• Allows interpretation of language in its social context | • Time-consuming to analyse
• Can 'read in' too much to the language used |

responds. Cohen and Manion (2004) describe a range of interviews from formal through informal to non-directive. Essentially, they are referring to the degree to which the interview is structured. *Structured interviews*, with a set of predefined questions, are administered as written by the interviewer. *Semi-structured interviews* will also have a predefined set of questions, however, the interviewer may vary the order of the questions or depart from this structure to ask additional questions. *Informal interviews* may involve areas of investigation rather than predefined questions, while non-directive interviews are likely to be led by the respondent. As a beginning researcher, you may feel more confident facing your respondent(s) with a set of preprepared questions, but you will need to decide whether it will be advantageous to vary these questions, or administer them as written. A reference back to your original research question(s) should help here.

When interviewing it is usual to tape-record and then transcribe your interviews. Note-taking is thought by some researchers to be insufficient to capture the detail of the interview and could, therefore, compromise the validity of your data. Beginning researchers often underestimate how long transcription can take, so ensure that you plan sufficient time for transcription prior to your data analysis.

Questionnaires

Questionnaires are a widely used procedure that can accumulate quantities of data relatively quickly. You want to get the opinions of a wide variety of people concerning the subject you are interested in; you have not got time to talk to all of them individually so, therefore, you formulate a few questions and invite people to answer them. Blaxter *et al.* (2001) indicate that the way in which you administer the questionnaires can impact on the quality of data collected. For example, questionnaires can be done standing with a clipboard in the street, posted out to participants, completed electronically and even conducted over the telephone. Blaxter *et al.* (2001) suggest that although face-to-face questionnaires are likely to achieve a higher response rate, they are far more time-consuming for the researcher to administer; postal questionnaires may provide a lower response rate, but the administration is minimal. However, there is a cautionary note, where there is no interaction between participant and researcher, participants may not provide full answers, and questions may be misunderstood; data can then be disappointing. Therefore, you must design and word your questionnaire carefully. Again, Blaxter *et al.* (2001) provide some useful advice. They suggest avoiding imprecise questions, using smaller, more simple questions and avoiding too many open questions that take a long time to answer fully. Where fixed answers are required, multiple choice responses or scales (for example strongly agree, agree, disagree, strongly disagree) might be used. Piloting or trying out your questionnaire before using it is a good idea. This will provide feedback about the precision of your questions and whether they will give the useful and valid data you hope for (see Chapter 7).

Focus groups

Focus groups allow for the gathering of in-depth data. The data generated can be rich because, unlike an interview, there are more participants. Viewpoints can be shared, reflected upon, responded to and developed, so that their individual responses can become sharper, and may be more frank and open.

However, you do need to consider how you will select your group and its make-up. Will you use single or mixed gender? Will you use friendship groups? If so, how will this affect the data you collect? As a researcher, are you new to the group or do you have a relationship already established? Again, how will this affect the data you collect?

The role of the researcher is crucial to the success of this method. You need to remember that you must provide a secure structure for the discussion or activity but also be able to let the group go off at a tangent while knowing how and when to return and reformulate their views back in line with the area of focus. You may need to emphasize a question here. You will also need to be able to ask supplementary questions to clarify or extend the responses given or perhaps draw other members of the group in.

Two important considerations with the handling of focus groups are:

- What if someone takes over? Should I stop them?
- What if no one talks?

It is important to address a more dominant member of the group, perhaps indirectly at first by inviting other opinions, but often you will need to set down some ground rules or encourage that person directly to let others speak. If the group is extremely reserved you need to have a plan for this; for example, you might relate the topic to something that they would be motivated by, such as a popular TV programme or work they have been doing in class. Be very encouraging of responses, smile and use positive and open body language. As the discussion opens up, then you can gradually withdraw your leadership. Using focus groups is very challenging, but an effective focus group where you have the balance of personalities and the right dynamic will provide you with some very interesting and rich data.

Observation

If you are going to use observation as a method, as before it is important you know the purpose. Observation as a method is used for recording behaviours that occur at a given time under a certain set of circumstances. For example, you may wish to record how children react to an activity you ask them to partake in and how they interact with each other. The tool of observation gives you the opportunity to stand back and watch. However, you do need to be aware that the events and behaviours are being seen through your eyes with your particular biases and your particular take on the events. The key, therefore, is to be as objective as possible and be aware of how your interpretation could clash with what is actually happening. Simco and Warin (1997) suggest that the use of video provides a mechanism to check interpretations with others as well as the consideration of non-verbal responses. This may be important data where behaviours are a focus of the study.

When considering the use of observation, ask yourself:

- Where will I be when conducting the observation?
- How will my presence affect the behaviour of participants?
- What steps will I take to ensure that my own biases do not get in the way of my interpretations of what I observe?

Your responses to such reflection will lend transparency to your research and contribute towards Denscombe's eighth ground rule – objectivity.

Discourse and conversation analysis

These are highly specialized methods that involve a great deal of understanding of language structures. Discourse analysis can be interpreted as exploring how language supports the construction of meaning. Discourse analysis considers the language used but also as Cohen and Manion (2004) point out, 'the social actions performed in them' (p. 214). Discourse researchers often consider the talk, its organization and the social context in which it takes place. Conversation analysis can be interpreted as exploring the interaction between your participants, and analysts using this method will often consider how talk makes things happen and how the wheels of meaning are set in motion. These terms are contested and interpreted in different ways and if you are considering using either of these methods, you must develop your understanding further, and Tonkiss (2000) gives some excellent advice in 'analysing discourse'. In order to carry out these methods successfully, you need to have a robust system for analysing the language, usually through a coding system. Mercer (1995) gives some useful advice and suggestions concerning the practical details of analysing language.

Methodologies

How do I choose the best method for the research I want to undertake? You may be hoping for a simple answer to this question but, unfortunately, it is more complex than that. Different methods produce different types of knowledge and, therefore, the method you use will spring from a deeper philosophical standpoint than just a random choice of methods. The methods discussed above might be combined or used within an overarching methodology. Silverman (2000) states that *'A methodology defines how one will go about studying a phenomenon'* (p. 79; our italic). He goes on to state that they *'cannot be true or false, only more or less useful'* (p. 79; our italic). Therefore, the 'best' method or combination of methods is dependent on your philosophical standpoint and the type of information you require to successfully investigate your research question.

When you think you have identified an appropriate method or combination of methods:

Ask yourself: *'Will my chosen method(s)'*:

- generate data pertinent to my original research question(s)?
- generate data that is reliable and valid (see Chapter 5)?
- be manageable in the context of both my time and the time of my respondents?
- take appropriate account of ethical issues (see Chapter 4)?

References

Blaxter, L., Hughes, C. and Tight, M. (2001) *How to Research.* Buckingham: Open University Press.

Bryman, A. (2001) *Social Research Methods.* Oxford: Oxford University Press.

Cohen, L. and Manion, L. (2004) *Research Methods in Education.* London: Routledge.

Denscombe, M. (2002) *Ground Rules for Good Research: A 10 Point Guide for Social Researchers.* Buckingham: Open University Press.

Edwards, A. and Talbot, R. (1999) *The Hard-pressed Researcher*, 2nd edn. Harlow: Pearson Education.

Mason, J. (2002) *Qualitative Researching*. London: Sage.

Mercer, N. (1995) *The Guided Construction of Knowledge.* Clevedon: Multilingual Matters.

Silverman, D. (2000) *Doing Qualitative Research.* London: Sage Publications.

Simco, N. and Warin, J. (1997) Validity in image-based research: an elaborated illustration of the issues, *British Education Research Journal*, 23(5): 661–72.

Tonkiss, F. (2000) *Analyzing Discourse*, in C. Seale (ed.) *Researching Society and Culture.* London: Sage Publications.

Further reading

Arksey, H. and Knight, P. (1999) *Interviewing for Social Scientists: An Introductory Resource with Examples.* London: Sage Publications.

Grey, D. (2004) *Doing Research in the Real World.* London: Sage Publications.

O'Leary, Z. (2004) *The Essential Guide to Doing Research.* London: Sage Publications.

Ritchie, J. and Lewis, J. (2003) *Qualitative Research Practice: A Guide for Social Science Students and Researchers.* London: Sage Publications.

8 Intervention, innovation and creativity in the classroom: using findings to improve practice

Adrian Copping and Dennis Howlett

In this chapter we aim to develop your understanding of:

- The need for Innovation and Creativity in the classroom
- How we might develop Creativity in the classroom
- How classroom-based research might be planned for and implemented in order to develop the curriculum and our own practice.

First, we begin by reminding you of the ideas that have prompted the government to develop new approaches to curriculum organization and classroom practice. Second, we consider the various options available to you that might help you to achieve these objectives. Finally, we have the opportunity to review and evaluate a recent project of this kind and offer this as a recent case study in curriculum intervention and classroom-focused research.

> We need a new approach because the challenges we all face are unprecedented.
>
> (DfES 1999)

Society is changing, as it always has, but the evidence is all around us that this change is now occurring at an ever increasing rate. Contributory factors include the variation in population demographics, the change in the nature of work and economics, and the ever increasing rise and development of new technologies. At the same time we are becoming increasingly aware that most local issues and problems have, in fact, a 'global dimension'. In order to keep pace with these changes and their effects on individuals and on society, we have to respond to the challenge and to do so in a way that addresses as many of these issues as possible. We are, it seems, learning the value of 'joined-up thinking'. Education is at the heart of our preparation for a changing world, and must respond to the need to provide individuals with the future skills that will enable them to be the 'innovative and independent thinkers of tomorrow' (DfES 1999).

We cannot predict with any degree of certainty the knowledge and the combination of skills that will be required by our children in the future. But we can provide them with the appropriate attitudes and skills that will serve them best whatever their needs. That is to say, we can help them to develop a framework for thinking and a general approach to lifelong learning that will assist them now and help prepare them for the future, whatever that might hold.

It is the recognition that we are in some respects preparing for an unknown future that has prompted the shift in perspective to view education as a continuous life-long process. It does not end for the child as the last school bell rings, and it does not end for the teacher when the graduation ceremony closes.

If education is to be a life-long process, then it is as well that we are now looking at ways to make it both excellent and enjoyable as 'children learn best when they are excited and engaged – but what excites and engages those best is truly exciting teaching' (DfES 2003).

The findings of educational and social research from a wide variety of sources, including classroom-focused studies, have at last begun to unite and provide us with a coherent picture and, consequently, a new direction. The separate tributaries are beginning to form a single stream. The findings, being so widely based, are influencing government policy on social and educational issues. Indeed, one of the significant changes is the recognition that these two elements must be seen as a whole. This has caused among other things a fresh approach to curriculum organization, which at its heart recognizes the need for creativity and innovation.

Creative teaching is not new but it is being recognized and promoted as a means of satisfying, at once, all the varying needs and demands of recent government guidelines.

Creative teaching can itself take many forms, though these are not surprisingly, interrelated and mutually supportive. These include:

1   creative teaching;
2   creative thinking;
3   creative curriculum integration.

Creative teaching encourages us to employ a freer, more open, innovative approach in our classroom organization and our teaching. This is likely to be more inclusive and at the same time it will help provide the crucial, intrinsic motivation that is so important both in the short and long term. After all our ultimate goal is to achieve *life-long learners*; that is to say, individuals with the propensity and ability to go on learning and adjusting to the changing needs of a dynamic society.

According to DfES, 'teaching creatively involves teaching using imaginative approaches to make learning more interesting, exciting and effective' (1999). Creative thinking encourages us to develop a broader range of thinking skills and to teach these explicitly. They are to become the *focus* of our lessons and not simply something that somehow diffuses into the children because of their engagement in some other task. At times the development of these skills should be the main event and not the side-show. In particular, this would mean allowing the children to develop their creative thinking skills. The research and subsequent development of Guilford's (1967) work has shown us that we can and do adopt different frameworks for our thinking. Both of these are of value and both have their place. These are usually thought of as convergent or divergent thinking or more commonly as critical and creative thinking. It has long been the tradition of western education to prioritize the development of one of these forms of thinking over the other. We have rewarded and nurtured the rational, analytical form and largely ignored, or at worst suppressed the intuitive or creative approach.

While critical thinking is, of course, extremely useful and necessary, we are beginning to acknowledge that many of our greatest advances in the sciences as well as the arts are the result of creative thinking. This way of thinking will become even more important in the world of tomorrow. In order to help each individual learner to develop all forms of intelligence, and appropriate thinking frameworks, we must promote and nurture critical and creative thinking. Thus, the needs of the individual and society are both being met if we adopt this strategy. The immediate benefit as research has shown (Craft 2001) is that this is very likely to increase self-esteem, motivation and not, surprisingly, achievement. The long-term benefit is that we are laying the foundations for our life-long learners who are more likely to be both willing and able to seek out and solve future as yet unknown problems.

Creative integration allows an 'Innovative' approach to the organization of the curriculum as a whole. This will allow, where appropriate, a natural integration of areas of learning to their mutual benefit. It serves to reinforce the associated skills and concepts while at the same time offering a more realistic view of the future need for problem-solving skills. It will also encourage the more efficient use of expertise and associated partnership agencies.

Of course, we need to recognize and safeguard the individuality and integrity of each subject, but at the same time we should recognize that they are not mutually exclusive and that, in fact, they often have much in common.

This is true not only in terms of content but, more importantly, in terms of the attitudes and skills that they hold in common. Paradoxically, as we reap the benefits of allowing the boundaries to overlap, we become more aware of how the different 'subjects' bring their own unique perspective to our studies and to our problem-solving.

Thus, we can, for a while at least, reintegrate our knowledge and our approach to problem-solving in a more holistic way. The world has learnt to its cost that a narrow focus on important issues fails to recognize the repercussions of our actions. This broader view not only helps us to a deeper understanding, but helps us to see the many sides of any issue that we might need to take into account. It is a rehearsal, therefore, for the future when we come to understand things more completely as we are able to view them from a number of perspectives, especially when many issues may well have a multidimensional component.

Once again there are a number of ways to achieve some form of integration depending on the needs of the schools and any particular area of study. Fogarty (1991) has tabulated many of the forms this might take. We could, for instance, seek to integrate the entire curriculum or simply those aspects of it that at the moment are crying out to join forces. According to QCA (2003) 'the curriculum is more than areas and subjects; it is the totality of experiences' (2003).

As we develop these new approaches at the authority level and within individual schools, it would be very useful for our own professional development and for the benefit of our colleagues to ascertain whether our interventions and innovations have been successful in achieving our aims. That is to say the short-term aims and objectives of developing knowledge and skills and perhaps arriving at some worthwhile end product, together with our long-term aims of promoting life-long learners and creative and innovative thinkers through what is felt to be, by all participants, both excellent and enjoyable.

This reflection on our planning and practice and its evaluation as a positive innovation will allow us to gradually develop our approach and our techniques. By making it sufficiently rigorous and efficiently reported, this classroom-based research can be shared with colleagues and contribute towards our professional dialogue and collaboration, as mentioned in Chapters 2 and 3.

You will be continuing in your own quest as a life-long learner to improve your own practice and your own enjoyment in your chosen profession. You might come to understand a little more of how these ideas might be put into practice, and how you might organize your own classroom-based research, as you study the next section of this chapter. Here we offer you a recent case study of an example of innovative teaching and classroom-focused research in order that you can reflect on the planning, organization and outcome. At the same time we offer some useful planning frameworks that may guide your initial planning.

Case Study 1

Example of school-based research in practice

(A one-week saturation placement – PGCE primary)

The case study example is a one-week saturation placement taking place on our full-time primary PGCE course prior to the students' final placement. The aim of the week is to give the students an opportunity to work collaboratively and co-operatively with peers and school-based colleagues in a different way. We encourage students who, free of all constraints of being assessed, can plan an exciting, dynamic and engaging week of work based around a theme. The planning is done collaboratively between the schools and the students, and it provides a tremendous opportunity for students to bring in their specialist expertise, for example media, art, ICT, outdoor education and take control of the curriculum. The menu should proclaim a feast of cross-curricular delights, making meaningful links to learning across the curriculum and utilizing some of the learning themes that the Primary National Strategy's *'Excellence and Enjoyment, learning and teaching in the primary years'* brings to our attention: 'enquiry, creative thinking, evaluation, managing feelings, problem solving, empathy, reasoning, self awareness, motivation, information processing, communication, social skills' (DfES 2004: 6).

Historically, the success of the placement has been in the planning. As six of our partnership schools take part in the placement and we leave the school organization to them, the planning systems are not laid out centrally. Therefore, we have six different schools operating in six different ways. In order to fully capitalize on the opportunities presented in such a week as this, strong cohesive planning is essential.

> This is not just about learning and teaching opportunities but also about research. If research is going to improve our practice, then it needs to be planned and a focus needs to be identified.

Reflection on Case Study 1

From the inception of a creative, cross-curricular week, practitioner research opportunities need to be identified so that the opportunity holds more than an innovative learning experience for the children but also one for you. Figure 8.1 shows a suggested example of a starting point 'whole school planning framework' that can be adapted or used verbatim and provides some thinking prompts towards capitalizing on these opportunities. This is followed by a framework to be used alongside it supporting research opportunities (see Figure 8.2).

Ask yourself:

- Before my placement begins do I know what methods I will use to gather data?
- Do I know when I will conduct the data-gathering process?
- Is this manageable?

The climate of teaching in the primary school is changing. Many classes have a teaching team rather than one teacher in central charge of learning. The team teaching element of this theme week is a central part to capitalize on the opportunities presented. A team can best meet individual needs of learners, can observe children's responses to teaching styles and can support the teacher and learners in their activities. The contribution of all members of the team is vital in improving practice. Although the students were largely wary of this approach, as it was a bit different, many gained considerably from working in teams. (*Note: all names used are pseudonyms.*)

> *Shakila*: It gave me an opportunity to observe children.
> *Nick*: I could see how the children would respond.
> *Sam*: I could take aspects of someone else's practice and incorporate the bits the children liked into my own teaching. It was great getting tips and ideas from other people working with the same kids.

Time when you are not in the spotlight in a traditional teacher deliverer role is essential so that reflection and observation can occur. If these opportunities are not planned into a teacher's day, then the auto-

School Mission Statement	Central Theme	Global Dimensions

Aims and Objectives	
National Curriculum	**Other aspects of learning**
	e.g. Enjoyment, Creativity, Empathy

Which subjects are to be integrated?	**Appropriate Form of Integration** *How would you link up subjects and areas of learning most effectively?*	How will the subjects be integrated?

	Core activities	**Partnership with externals**
FS		
Y1		
Y2		
Y3		
Y4		
Y5		
Y6		

Figure 8.1: A suggested framework for planning cross-curricular theme work

Research Focus	
What will you find out?	
• Children	
• Staff	
• Technique	
• Organization	

Data Collection Methods	
How will you find it out?	
• Questionnaire	
• Evaluation of Product	
• Observation	
N.B. This is not an exhaustive list	

Designing Your Method	
• Type of questions	
• A focus group?	
• Administration	

Analysing Your Data	
What does it tell you?	
How you go about your analysis will depend on your question and method.	
You may have quantitative and qualitative elements.	

Implications for Practice	
What will you do as a result?	
• Teaching style?	
• Resources?	
• Organization?	
• Curriculum?	
• Can any of your findings be disseminated?	

Figure 8.2: A suggested framework for planning classroom research

pilot of systemized responses and reversion to delivering a worksheet-based curriculum happens and we do not move forward as professionals. When undertaking your own research project ask yourself:

- Am I using my 'non-teaching time' effectively to reflect and observe my own and other practice?
- What impact will this have?
- How can other adults best support the learning and teaching when I am leading the lesson?

The outcomes of this theme week opportunity have been varied and positive. The thought of putting between 30 and 35 students into six schools and asking them to work in teams of 3–5 that included the class teacher seemed a tall order not only to us but also to the students and, of course, the schools involved. The schools volunteered to be involved and we selected six of our forefront partnership schools, some of them held training school status at the time. The outcomes for them were very positive. One school involved the local press, a video company and a local transport company and strengthened links with their community significantly. Other schools found that the collaboration required forced their staff to become more cohesive and galvanized and many through reflection and observation have taken on 'more risky' ideas into their general teaching. School evaluations have used the word 'energized' repeatedly to describe the effects on their staff and learning and teaching in the school. The children who have been involved, many for several years since the project began, have experienced different learning opportunities, cultures, media and attempted things they never dreamed possible in a traditional school environment. Teachers have commented on the smiling faces in the classrooms, a greater desire to participate than in a 'traditional' school day and the general buzz around school. The children, too, have valued the extra adults in the school, as one particular child commented:

Rahima aged 8: It was great having more teachers, it felt like I mattered and I was picked to say something when I'm not normally.

When undertaking your research in school, ask yourself:

- What contribution is this making to the children's learning?
- What benefit does this have for the whole school?
- What wider contexts could your research be situated in beyond the course you are studying?

Many of the students only saw the benefits later on. Although the majority enjoyed the week, many felt little benefit at the time due to pressure of planning for their final placement, applying for jobs and finishing essays. Some, in fact, felt that it got in the way of the more serious business of passing the course. However, given time to reflect, the outcomes were tangible and positive for most of them. Some found planning for a week rather than individual lessons useful in shaping vision, ideas and product; others found looking at the curriculum and learning experience more holistically something to take away, and others found the complex business of working as a team a hugely valuable experience to take away with them. Many also found that planning and carrying out a peer observation, both as observer and observed, was a valuable and growing experience. Some students shared that although they felt threatened at the time, the feedback was supportive and helpful and that their practice had improved through it. Some even went further and shared that doing a peer observation had changed the way that they thought about being formally observed by their class teacher and school-based mentor on their future placements and into their newly qualified year.

Ask yourself:

- How can you as a developing professional gain from the experience of researching classroom practice? What do you hope to gain from it?

Where, then, does the research fit in? We had planned this research opportunity with Years 4, 5 and 6 in two of the participating schools and asked the students to invite the children to participate in a short questionnaire by asking them about the activities that they had enjoyed, why they had enjoyed them, whether they preferred an integrated cross-curricular day and whether they saw and could identify any links between learning in different curriculum subjects. We also asked class teachers to record their observations of the quality of the learning that the children had engaged in over the week. The purpose of this was to look at the impact that a cross-curricular approach, and a less constricting organization of the curriculum, had on children's engagement with, and quality of, learning. We received 82 responses in total and they are recorded in Table 8.1. We chose to tabulate these results in this way because we wanted to group the responses and then be able to compare the amount of responses given to each category. This was a useful tool to help draw out some recommendations from the data. It is not always necessary or appropriate to tabulate results in this way.

Table 8.1: Activities that the children enjoyed the best

Activities that the children enjoyed best		Responses	%
'Hands on' in the environment activities		27	33
Creative art		15	18
Sport (games)		10	12
Creative dance		9	11
Relevant 'job' type work		8	10
Design technology		7	9
Learning a new skill		6	7
Reasons for enjoying them			
A personal like		18	21
Fun		14	16
Created a tangible outcome		9	11
There were short, sharp and various activities		7	9
Teachers trusted pupils with tools and apparatus		5	5
A new experience		3	4
Problem-solving		3	4
A chance to get dirty		3	4
No one argued (positive environment created)		3	4
Got the chance to use a variety of materials		3	4
Already had a good skill level at the activity		3	4
It was a challenge		3	4
The activities promoted health and well-being		3	4
Relevant learning		2	2
Group work		2	2
The activities were simple to do		1	1
Pupils who preferred an integrated day	Yes	78	95
to a normal day	No	4	5
Pupils who could see how activities	Yes	26	32
from subjects linked in terms of	No	14	17
knowledge, skills and understanding	Some	42	51

Ask yourself:

- How will you select, classify and organize the data you have gathered?
- Is it appropriate to tabulate it?
- What information can be gained from it?
- What is the purpose of presenting your data in this way?

See Chapter 10 and 11 for further guidance concerning data analysis and writing up results.

From this assimilation of responses from the children, some interesting observations and analysis can be made. This is the purpose of the research: to use these observations to inform future practice both at a classroom and possible school level. First of all, over 50 per cent of the children enjoyed 'hands-on' activities where they could be free of chairs, tables and worksheets and enjoy creative arts activities, where they could express themselves through a variety of media. Nearly 50 per cent enjoyed them because they were fun and motivating, something they personally liked and created a tangible outcome. Instantly, this simple analysis begins to answer questions about children's lack of motivation in 'traditional' school activities that can largely revolve around an activity designed for manageability, control and because it meets the learning objective. These responses tell us that children like to be physically engaged in their environment, get their hands dirty and express themselves creatively. Where is this in the learning opportunities we provide for our children? Researching our practice and the children's responses leads us to ask significant questions about our practice, promoting further discussion, reflection and ultimately change.

The next observation is in the variety of responses to why children enjoyed the activities. From this, the children engaged with the activities for a variety of reasons from an interpersonal perspective, the classroom was a happier place, to feeling confident with a different activity because actually it was not that difficult in terms of prior knowledge and skill requirements, to the fact that we did not have to spend ages on the same activity. Clearly, we would not be advocating that children should never be challenged and should never do any sustained activity, but questions can again be raised about the purpose of the activity and learning that is being undertaken, and are the children learning something more than just skills and knowledge? Perhaps they are learning empathy, team work, how to discuss, how to disagree with someone, how to respond personally. Another interesting observation is that the children felt that they were given trust with materials and apparatus and they clearly valued that. Questions here could be asked about how many ideas do we as teachers have but do not take forward because of nagging doubts about children handling certain resources and tools?

When classifying your own data ask yourself:

- What themes emerge from the data?
- Are there any overwhelming responses? If so, what could the reasons be for that?
- What does your data tell you and does it prompt any further questions for discussion?

There was an overwhelmingly affirmative response to an integrated cross-curricular day. Some in particular stand out:

> *Aasima age 11*: I like the school week like this week because it was a fun and there were challenges, we learnt new things.
>
> *Sarah age 8*: It is so much more fun than a normal day.

Interestingly, a small percentage of the children saw no links between subjects. Many saw some links and were able to identify how elements of understanding in literacy, for example, had supported geography work, or how making masks in art had contributed to a cultural understanding of an African tribe.

As teachers, our concern should be about ensuring that all pupils in our care fulfil their potential and participate in the most effective learning experience that they possibly can. Therefore, questions raised from this simple research into the impact of a cross-curricular approach and a less constricting organization of the curriculum should be discussed in order for learning and teaching to be improved throughout the school. Some important questions that need consideration arising from research are:

- How can we incorporate more creative arts and 'hands-on' learning into our school curriculum?
- How can we respond to some of the reasons children enjoy activities to ensure that there is a greater participation in learning?
- Can we organize our curriculum in such a way so as to encourage more cross-curricular, relevant and contextualized learning opportunities?

Remember that your research project is about informing your practice but it may raise some issues for the school. Ask yourself:

- What can you take from it to inform your practice?
- How can you share your findings, if appropriate with the school, sensitively and helpfully?

This small-scale piece of practitioner research has raised some important questions to reflect on what can and should improve our practice as teachers. This chapter has considered the need for innovation and creativity in the classroom to ensure that more effective learning opportunities are created and that more children are participating in meaningful and relevant learning. By thinking about education as more than an hour of English, an hour of maths, a slot for science and half an hour a week for the foundation subjects, we start to think about children, how they learn, what they need and how they respond to the world of the twenty-first century. We need to be teaching them to learn, providing opportunities for them to do it in ways in which they can engage with. In order to do this we must think about our practice, reflect on how the children respond to an activity, to our teaching style and approach, and in so doing we engage in practitioner research. These thoughts when they lead to action can prompt changes to our teaching, to the curriculum and its organization that can help our children be the *'innovative and independent thinkers of tomorrow'*. As one teacher commented:

> *Sue*: I had no idea that X could even think like that. It's opened my eyes and helped me see how children, that I'm ashamed to say I'd written off, engage, think and are creative. I was nearly in tears.

Bibliography

Copping, A. and Eady, S. (2006) Creativity outside convention: how a saturation placement can develop 21st century holistic teachers, in *Challenges and Opportunities: Developing Learning and Teaching in ITE across the UK*. Bristol: ESCalate.

Craft, A. (2001) *Analysis of Research and Literature on Creativity and Education*. London: QCA.

DfES (1999) *All our Futures: Creativity, Culture and Education*. London: DfES.

DfES (2003) *Excellence and Enjoyment: A Strategy for Primary School*. London: DfES.

DfES (2004) *Excellence and Enjoyment, learning and teaching in the primary Years*. London: DfES.

Fogarty, R. (1991) *The Mindful School: How to Integrate the Curricula*. Palatine: Skylight Publishing.

Guilford, J.P. (1967) *The Nature of Human Intelligence*. New York: McGraw-Hill.

QCA (2003) *Creativity, Find it! Promote It!* London: DfEE.

QCA (2005) *Creativity, Find it! Promote it! Practical Materials for Schools*. London: DfEE.

9   Collaborative research

Des Hewitt

Objectives

This chapter will help the reader understand:

- the nature of collaboration in research;
- a rationale for carrying out collaborative research;
- ways of carrying out collaborative research;
- different forms of collaborative research;
- case study examples of collaborative research from primary and secondary schools.

Introduction

In the earlier chapters you were introduced to some important concepts and methods in research. Collaboration with others is one of the most rewarding approaches to research. According to Brown

'The evidence indicates how teachers' involvement and confidence can be built in expansive learning environments characterised by specialist support, collaborative working, and the development of mutual trust' (2005: 402).

To some people *collaborative research* is an extension of professional conversation, reflection on practice or an important part of action research (Raymond and Leinenbach 2000). Parsons and Stephenson (2005) suggest that practitioners reflect on their professional practices most effectively when they do this with others. Ultimately, the process of developing knowledge is a social process (Kvale 2002). Collaborative research offers people involved in education the opportunity to investigate and improve their practice.

What is collaborative research?

I have taken care in this chapter to include people who are not teachers, as I would like to argue that collaborative research should go much further than just teachers investigating their own settings. The 'Every Child Matters' policy developments in England (DfES 2003) offers the opportunity for professionals from different disciplines (education, health, social care), different institutions (Integrated Children's Services, Sure Start and voluntary organizations) and, indeed, parents to contribute to improvements to the educational experience of children in schools. Collaborative research might look like the following:

- Two teachers in a secondary school investigating why pupils fail to generalize mathematical skills to science lessons.
- A history tutor of a local university working with trainee teachers and partnership primary schools to implement an out-of-school learning project in museums as part of a Creative Partnerships project.
- A lecturer at a further education college investigates behaviour in post-16 settings with the help of a 'Centre of Excellence' in a local university.
- A special school for children with speech and language difficulties works with a university to investigate the effectiveness of professional collaboration between speech and language therapists and teachers.
- A local authority works with a university to investigate barriers and aids for health, social care and educational professionals involved in providing integrated children's services.

A summary of some of these different types of collaborative research are listed below:

- Teachers working together to investigate relevant issues in their own school.
- Teachers from different schools working together.
- Teachers from a teacher education partnership working with support from the host university or training provider.
- Teachers working with national or international professional associations, government institutions or local government authorities.
- Teachers and other professionals working together on areas of common interest and concern.
- Teachers and parents working together to investigate an area of

concern or common interest. The Forest Schools movement originated in Denmark, but is now well established in some English primary and secondary schools. In this approach to the curriculum, schools work closely with bodies like the Forestry Commission to realign the curriculum. Lessons are linked to a forest or wooded area, often with the help of other members of the community to provide links to the environment. This should be an ongoing commitment rather than one-off visits, for example, to a forestry centre.

- Teachers and pupils working together to research an area of common interest as a part of the curriculum. The 'Mantle of the Expert' is one example of this approach to learning. Developed by the renowned drama teacher, Dorothy Heathcote, in this approach children operate as experts leading an extended project. This will often relate to the operation of an imagined business or organization. Children make decisions about how the project will develop and the teacher's role is more like a mentor.

Some theorists would discount the last two of the above examples as not constituting true examples of educational research. However, I would question this, since here there has been a significant focus on the role of pupil 'voice' and supporting parental involvement in schools. For instance, Baker's (2003) discussion of the role of parents in motivating struggling readers provides a very interesting account of how to promote effective parental involvement in home literacy. This project could have involved the collection of data by parents, but how much were they involved in framing the research questions? Arguably, to truly investigate the impact of parental support on struggling readers, it is important that parents contribute to the direction of the research, so that it represents their views on the problems and some of the solutions to encourage reading.

The following example in Case Study 1 illustrates quite an orthodox collaborative arrangement between a university and teachers in local schools as they investigate ways of developing children's writing.

Primary School Case Study 1

Developing Reflective Writers in Primary Schools: findings from partnership research

(Corden 2002)

Children are the ultimate beneficiaries of collaborative research into classroom learning. For instance, as a result of a collaborative research between teachers and a local university into the development of children's writing, one pupil (Billie), wrote in her journal:

> Before the TRAWL project I didn't really know many literary devices. I had no idea just how much they could improve a text or why they are used and what they can do. I hadn't looked for links between the beginning and end of my story before and I never knew where my stories were leading to. I thought it was wrong to borrow, copy or adapt ideas to make my story better. Now I know a lot about literary devices and what they do. I realise just how much they can improve my writing. I now know that adapting ideas off another person is alright and that lots of people do it.
>
> (Corden 2002: 273)

Research description

- Principal aims were to develop the quality of children's independent writing, metacognition, with children making conscious and deliberate decisions based on reason; and to develop children's self-esteem and confidence as young writers.
- Collaboration between 14 teachers, covering the Key Stage 2 age range (7–11) and colleagues from a university teacher education department.
- Over two school terms teachers observed and recorded each other during focused literacy sessions and writing workshops. The teachers attended preparatory and developmental meetings and, as a research group, met on a regular basis to discuss progress and evaluate data.
- Results suggest a significant increase in pupils' ability to engage with the process approach to writing. Their ability to reflect on their learning and their wider self-esteem also increased.

While Corden recognizes the very important impact on the children's learning, we should not forget the opportunity to work with others. He cites Wells's (1990) notion of a community of literature thinking as an outcome of imaginative and resourceful teachers. This project involved collaboration between university teacher educators and school teachers. This is quite a typical arrangement and is replicated by many other projects reported in the educational research literature.

Reflection on Case Study 1

- What opportunities are available to you to work with colleagues in local universities?
- What connections do you have with the university or college where you are studying or have studied?
- If you have trainee teachers on placement in your school, are there any opportunities to develop your own interests as part of the partnership?
- Corden's focus on children's writing emanates from a national concern about the quality of children's writing in English primary schools. By providing regular writing input for children, university tutors and teachers were able to work together to teach explicit literary technique while avoiding formulaic writing.
- The first step in developing collaborative research is to identify people who you would be happy to work with.
- University and school partnerships provide one of the strongest opportunities for you to resolve challenges provided by the classroom.

According to Sachs collaborative research is not an easy option.

> Collaborative inquiry is neither simple nor easy. Because it makes new demands of both communities of researchers it necessarily assumes an experimental aspect ... As a prime consideration for success of such endeavours it is important that neither partner asks the other to become the same as them. Instead, each partner needs to come to respect and appreciate the difference between them and the different roles they play in the education enterprise.
>
> (1999: 44)

An interesting feature of university/school collaborative research concerns the research question. I explained that the research question is an important starting point in developing any research, including collaborative research. Who develops the question? Is this a question that teachers suggest from their practice? Or is this a research project developed by a university tutor, principally for them to fulfil their annual research publication requirements? The worst example of this so-called collaborative research is where university supervisors publish their students' work under their own name with the minimum of collaborative input. Thankfully, I have rarely seen this approach in British universities. It does suggest that the power and status of collaborative parties is an important consideration. Negotiation and ownership of the research focus between the various parties are important prerequisites of successful collaborative research (Sachs 1999).

Christie (2007) in his discussion of collaboration, identifies an important distinction between:

- Collaboration: working together and influencing outcomes in a joint and purposeful way.
- Co-operation: working separately on a common project.

Collaboration and co-operation may occupy different points on the research continuum depending on the degree of power, control and status operated by the research participant. It is not to say that 'collaborative' research is any better than *'co-operative' research*. Some teachers may be happy to let a more experienced colleague or institution take the lead in a project. In fact, this may be a way to develop experience prior to understanding your own research. On the other hand, so-called collaborative research, which is nominally inclusive of all involved, is a sham and should be discouraged. Collaborative research that superficially aims to investigate the classroom without really considering the perspective of the classroom practitioner is probably not valid nor reliable (Kvale 2002).

Why carry out research?

All research should start with a question. Normally this question focuses on a professional area of interest or concern. The question often starts with a wh-question word:

- What is ...?
- How can we ...?
- Why is ...?
- Where is the most effective ...?
- When is the best time to ...?

Collaborative research might start with one person asking themselves a question. They might then recruit other people to the germ of a collaborative research project. In other cases, friends in a work setting might want a collaborative research project as a vehicle to support their professional working relationship. Teachers can see collaborative research as a career progression, i.e. carry out a collaborative piece of research with a local university with the hope of obtaining a job! In other countries, teachers' pay is linked to formal professional development. In this country the new Standards for Classroom Teachers (TDA 2007) provide opportunities for teachers to work with other less experienced colleagues in investigating and disseminating their findings. There are, therefore, a host of reasons for teachers to take an interest in collaborative research.

There are many definitions of collaborative research and reasons for encouraging it:

- *Collaborative inquiry* occurs when teacher educators and practising teachers engage in a process of collaboration that articulates academic research and practitioner research (Sachs 1999).
- *Collaborative research* can involve teachers in 'theory seeking' and 'theory testing' (Corden 2002).
- *Research partnerships* promotes critical thinking as a way of restructuring existing understandings and developing as existing practitioners.
- Collaborative projects can promote professional learning and professional renewal.
- Collaborative research differs from *reflective practice* in that the former should be grounded in data that has been systematically collected and analysed for defined purposes (Sachs 1999: 42).
- Collaborative inquiry lies in a continuum that includes reflective practice, professional development, formal qualifications and more formal research projects.

There can be professional barriers between university academics and teaching professionals. On the one hand, teachers can be afraid of the so-called academic 'theory', dismissing it as irrelevant to everyday practice, whereas academics can reject insights provided by the classroom practitioner as lacking a rationale and merely implementing government doctrine. The reality, of course, is that universities and schools have their own cultures. Collaboration is difficult where professionals feel threatened by outsiders who claim to be experts in an area where the development of theory could be seen as denying the validity of one's own practice (Sachs 1999). University colleagues have a responsibility, therefore, to promote links that encourage trust. Since all practice in school is predicated on some kind of theory and all teacher education is linked to some kind of practice, there is every chance that schools and universities can negotiate mutually beneficial research opportunities.

Secondary School Case Study 2

Promoting group talk and higher-order thinking in pupils by 'coaching' secondary English trainee teachers

(Sutherland 2006)

Collaborative research can often provide answers to resolve a gap between the rhetoric of government policy and the reality of the classroom learning. One such example is in the promotion of group talk in secondary schools (Sutherland 2006):

These studies indicate firstly, that pupils often sit in groups, but work individually, providing little evidence of rich, 'exploratory' talk, characterised by collaborative reasoning (Barnes and Todd, 1977; refined by Mercer et al., 1999); secondly, that pupils often see completion of a task, not the process of talking as the key objective; thirdly, that their talk is often constrained by their anticipation of teacher evaluation; and fourthly, that there is a gap in professional training for teachers in group work, leaving them unaware of the complexity of this area, yet unconfident about their skills.

(Sutherland 2006: 106)

Research description

- Six trainee teachers from a secondary English PGCE programme from five schools were given additional training in developing group talk and higher-order thinking skills.
- The trainee teachers helped Year 7 English classes in developing exploratory talk. They did this by using explicit ground rules created by the pupils ('include everyone', 'give reasons', 'ask for explanations'). Teachers also used 'low control' moves to encourage independent exploratory talk for learning.
- Trainees were actively involved in planning, implementing and evaluating the learning, which was tape-recorded so that detailed transcriptions of the talk could be used for content analysis. It is not clear, however, whether the trainees or their mentors were involved in the transcription and analysis of the activities. This is significant because this can be an extremely time-consuming aspect of any research.
- Trainees and pupils felt that pupils spoke more, displayed

increased confidence and wrote more effectively as a result of the positive impact of their use of exploratory talk.
- One very interesting result of the involvement of teacher mentors in the project was the impact of the novice trainee teachers on more expert practitioners:

One teacher observed, a month after the end of the project, continuing the model, said: 'The ground rules and the search for a suitably challenging task have been incredibly useful [...] It's made me look again at group work and reflect more deeply on how precisely to do it.'

(Sutherland 2006: 112)

Reflection on Case Study 2

- Collaborative research can provide useful resources for recording, processing and analysing data. However, participants should ask themselves if it would be useful for them to be involved at all stages of the research methodology. If not, can the research be considered to be fully collaborative?
- Strauss and Corbin (1998) talk about the process of 'saturating oneself in the data' and producing insights through an active process to generate 'grounded theory'. By not taking part in the processing and analysis of data, do participants risk becoming marginalized from the research?
- Mentors of trainee teachers can benefit greatly from the research carried out by their students. Most undergraduate students on teacher training programmes carry out an independent study of some kind. This provides an opportunity for mentors and trainees to work together on an area of interest. While there will be ethical and professional reasons to ensure that a student carries out and submits their own work, there is no reason why mentor and trainee collaborative research interests should not coincide.

How to carry out collaborative research

The following factors are often considered to be essential in promoting positive outcomes in collaborative research:

- Negotiation of research focus and questions by all collaborators.
- Regular communication between research participants to ensure a shared understanding of the original and developing focus.
- An emphasis on the personal and professional development of teachers and teacher educators rather than just producing resources.
- Collegial and collaborative approaches and a system of critical friends to review and trial early drafts of all materials and to advise on their development.
- Active participation and critical reflection to assist teacher educators to clarify the strengths and limitations of their present practice; and to establish their personal ownership of the project.
- Transparency in the management and use of resources, time and money (where the research is separately funded).

The above principles are important for any collaborative project. But only you can decide on the quality and extent of any collaborative research. Remember that your original research, focus is likely to change as your ideas develop. In collaborative research the more people you work with the more dynamic your research, is likely to be. Research projects are never the same at the end compared to the beginning!

The following questions will help you to design a collaborative research project. I have avoided repeating steps that any research project will consider but the following provide some insight into the collaborative element to the research:

Research inception

- Who will be involved in the collaborative research?
- Who will contribute the design and planning of the research as collaborators?
- Who will collect the data?
- Which people will provide the data, that is who will be the subjects of the research?
- What will be the respective roles of the research collaborators?
- What are the commitment and motivations of the research collaborators?

Research planning

- Will everyone be able to contribute the same amount of time to the research. If not, have you all agreed on the respective commitments?
- What are the risks of researchers dropping out of the project, and what will you all do if this happens?
- Has the research framework been designed with the expectations for the involvement of each researcher in mind?
- What arrangements have been made for involving everyone in the project and keeping them up to date on the development of the research?

Research governance

- Who takes responsibility for ensuring that the research meets project deadlines, outcomes and management of resources?
- Where difficulties occur, what procedures do you all have in place for dealing with these?
- Have your respective employers/institutions given you permission to carry out the research?

Research focus, aims, scope and limitations

- What are your agreed research focus/question and subsidiary questions?
- Does everyone have the same understanding of the research focus and scope?
- If this changes over the period of the research, has everyone agreed to this?

Literature review

- Is it possible to delegate a search of the relevant literature to different members of the research team?
- Have you all agreed a common way of recording and sharing useful information from the literature search, especially in recording references?
- Do all participants use terms and concepts in the same way in your research?

Research approach and methodology

- Have you all agreed on the 'feel' for your research: remember, once you decide on a qualitative, quantitative or mixed approach, this will have an ongoing impact on the nature of the research process and outcomes?
- Who will carry out which part of the research methodology?
- How will you ensure that different people will collect data in the same way and, therefore, that reliability is ensured?
- In analysing the research data, how have you ensured that this data is carried out consistently by different people and that the interpretation of the results is not affected by the various ideological positions of the research participants?
- Are the subjects of your research happy to work with all the researchers? You have a duty to provide details of all the researchers to ensure that you have informed consent.

Research report

- Interpretation of the results of any research must be agreed by all those involved in a research project. Have you a mechanism for reconciling any disagreements about interpretation of the data?
- While it may not be possible to write the research report together, have you ensured that all participants have had the opportunity to review, agree and, where appropriate, revise the report?

Research dissemination

- Have you planned for equity in the contributions for research participants in the dissemination of the research?
- Where the researchers come from different professional backgrounds, does the approach to dissemination take account of the different purposes and audiences involved?

While there cannot be a template for all forms of collaborative research, I have found the above principles to be useful in avoiding the pitfalls of collaborative research. Goldstein (2000) provides a useful warning to those involved in designing collaborative research:

> Given my superficial awareness of the balance of power problems that often mar research relationships, a problem referred to gently as 'impositional tendencies' (Lather, 1991)

and strongly as 'conceptual imperialism' (Stanley & Wise, 1983), I believed that I had designed our study to be a partnership in which both of us had something to offer and both of us had something to gain. Martha offered me the opportunity to do my research in her classroom: I had a lot to gain from that. I overlooked any way that my presence might have complicated Martha's teaching life, unaware that 'no matter how welcome, even enjoyable, the field-worker's presence may appear to "natives" fieldwork still represents an intrusion'.

(Goldstein 2000: 522)

The following example provides a salutary insight for all those involved in government-funded teacher collaborative research.

Primary/Secondary School Case Study 3

A comparison of the teaching of reading in Year 6 and Year 7
(Hewitt and Mellor 1998)

Collaborative research does not have to involve universities or initial teacher education. For several years, the Department for Education and Skills and the Teacher Training Agency have sponsored research by teachers into their own practice. Many of these have involved groups of practitioners investigating their own practices. Hewitt and Mellor (1998) was one such example.

Research description

- The research aimed to investigate the reaching of reading in a Year 6 and a Year 7 English class.
- Teachers and pupils were observed by teacher researchers in each of the classes. A semi-structured interview was carried out to discuss the teachers' perceptions of the strategies used to encourage successful reading.
- Observations and interviews were transcribed and analysed by the researchers.
- Teachers in Year 6 were seen to have a focus on both literature and language, while in Year 6 there was a much greater focus on the interpretation of literature: concentrating on text level features rather than word and sentence level features.

Reflection on Case Study 3

- The researchers on this project received funding from the Teacher Training Agency under the Best Practice Research Grant scheme. This provided financial support to allow time away from the classroom to carry out the research. Do you have access to any similar such funding?
- Bids from collaborative groups for funding can be well received where they demonstrate a more effective use of public funds: addressing wider research concerns and having a wider professional impact in a more economical way.
- A requirement of funding by the Teacher Training Agency was to prepare a short information leaflet to disseminate details of the research. An interesting outcome of this process was that previously qualitative information was edited and turned into quantitative information by the publisher of this short report. While this did not detract from the conclusions of the report, researchers should be wary about how their research is to be used and disseminated.

Different forms of collaborative research

Government-sponsored 'practitioner research' has been the focus of many recent developments (Brown 2005). There has been a raft of new professional networks and practitioner best practice opportunities:

- Primary National Strategy professional networks.
- TDA Best Practice Research grants.
- Professional internet resources such as Multi-verse (www. multiverse.ac.uk) which, in part, sponsors some research into the areas of equality and diversity in education.
- Escalate (HEFCE-sponsored organization for research and development in teacher education).
- Partnership Project (TDA-funded opportunities to research and develop initial teacher education). This frequently involved school and university partnerships in developing their practices.

Funding always generates another dimension to any collaboration research. Not enough money can create a feeling that goodwill is being stretched. Significant resources could lead to the research being seen as an opportunity for income generation. The TDA and DfES grants have suffered from this latter dimension. For the best of intentions, the government has sought to sponsor genuine research for the benefit of practitioners. Both universities and schools have in some cases used the funding to support other areas of their provision. There is nothing like money to generate friction in any collaborative arrangement!

While professional and partnership networks can provide opportunities for collaborative research, it is important to recognize that the characteristics of collaborative research may vary. For instance, Ritchie and Rigano (2007: 131) discuss the various types of collaborative research:

- *Distributed collaboration* is a widespread and the most casual pattern. Similar interests link members in a distributed collaboration where conversations at times may lead to personal insights or even arguments. Distributed collaborations can form and dissolve quickly in such contexts as conferences, working groups or committees, and online discussion forums.
- *Complementarity collaboration* is the most practised form of collaboration that is based on complementarity of expertise, disciplinary knowledge, roles and temperament. It is characterized by a division of labour that frequently realizes in mutual appropriation or the stretching of human possibilities of partners at both intellectual and emotional levels after sustained engagement.
- *Family collaborations* involve flexible or evolving roles that are frequently intense engagements that cannot be sustained indefinitely. Usually in dyads, partners can help each other shift roles and, like family members, can 'take over for each other while still using their complementarity'.
- *Integrative collaboration* requires prolonged periods of committed activity by partners. In some cases the participants construct a common set of beliefs, or ideology, which sustains them in periods of opposition or insecurity. Partners in an integrative collaboration can experience a profound sense of bonding or solidarity during the creation of a new vision through successful interactions.

Fien *et al.* (2001) provide a very good example of the last of the above in their 'Learning for a sustainable environment' project. This action research network provided teachers across the Asia-Pacific region with the opportunity to develop practices in a participatory model of research. This was framed in contrast to the 'cult of the expert' approach to research. While the project provided opportunities to develop planning, teaching and resources for sustainable development, the authors saw 'the power and potential of the action research network as a relatively low cost, region-wide and egalitarian approach to educational change' (Fien *et al.* 2001: 220). While not all collaborative research is likely to meet such ambitious criteria, collaborative researchers should recognize the importance of the 'research journey' as well as 'research outcomes'. Sometimes the journey is as important as reaching the destination itself!

Glossary

collaborative inquiry   this is a subtle distinction to demarcate the coming together of professional and academic insight (for instance teachers and university lecturers) to discuss questions and issues of common interest. Inquiry importantly does not imply that there is a 'researched' evidence base in the traditional sense.

collaborative research   the collection of some kind of evidence to answer questions set by two or more individuals, often building on research theory or models of practice previously developed by others. Truly collaborative research involves equality of participation through-out the phases of research, including data collection and analysis. This could involve teachers, teaching assistants, pupils, students and parents.

complementarity collaboration   the research collaborators may well 'play to their strengths' by adopting different roles according to the varying expertises of the group. Negotiation of the varying roles is important if power and status are not to be abused.

co-operative research   cooperation implies working together, whereas collaboration implies a more active process of negotiating the research focus, methodology and outcomes. In fact, collaborative research suggests that the definition and negotiation of validity in the research is shared.

distributed collaboration   the most common form of collaboration, this is less intense than a 'family collaboration' in that the 'collaborators' may take on roles for a limited duration according to the needs of the research: coming into or leaving the research as is necessary.

family collaboration   working like a family, often taking on different roles according to the strengths of the individuals, collabora-tors' roles will evolve. Sometimes in intense periods of activity, which are not sustainable over the long term, the roles of the collaborators may change according to the needs of the research.

integrative collaboration this involves prolonged periods of intense collaboration over a long period of time. In this situation the collaborators are sustained by a common focus, set of ideals and beliefs that sustain the collaborators in the face of any tensions and barriers.

reflective practice professionals consider ways of acting before, during or after an activity. It might involve developing insights into perceived problems, offering alternatives or evaluations of adopted practice. This can be a relatively opaque and personal activity or may be formalized through discussion, the use of certain thinking tools or professional mechanisms for developing explicit and conscious investigation of practice. This does not involve the development of a conscious evidence base of data collected with a systematic research methodology.

research governance this describes the structures and processes for taking responsibility for decision making in research. In collaborative research this can be empowering of the collaborators or it can lead to an imposition of ideas by a more powerful individual on another.

References

Baker, L. (2003) The role of parents in motivating struggling readers, *Reading and Writing*, 19(1): 87–106.

Barry, D. and Todd, F. (1977) Communication & Learning in Small groups. London: Routledge and Keegan Paul.

Brown, S. (2005) How can research inform ideas of good practice in teaching? The contributions of some official initiatives in the UK, *Cambridge Journal of Education*, 35(3): 383–405.

Christie, D. (2007) Collaborating to learn and learning to collaborate. Keynote speech at the Escalate Annual Conference, St Martin's College, Lancaster, 18 May 2007.

Corden, R. (2002) Developing reflective writers in primary schools: findings from partnership research, *Educational Review*, 54(3): 250–76.

DfES (2003) *Every Child Matters*. London: DfES Green Paper.

Fien, J., Kumar, P. and Ravindranath, M.J. (2001) An action research network as a strategy for educational change: the 'learning for a sustainable environment' project, *Journal of Educational Change*, 2: 207–21.

Goldstein, L. (2000) Ethical dilemmas in designing collaborative research: lessons learned the hard way, *International Journal of Qualitative Studies in Education*, 13(5): 517–30.

Hewitt, D. and Mellor, L. (1998) *A Case Study of Reading in Years 6 and 7*. London: Teacher Training Agency.

Kvale, S. (2002) The social construction of validity, in N.K. Denzin and Y.S. Lincoln (eds) *The Qualitative Inquiry Reader*. London: Sage Publications.

Lather, P. (1991) *Getting Smart: Feminist Research and pedagogy with/in the Post Modern*. New York: Routledge.

Mercer, N., Wegerif, R. and Dawes, L. (1999) Children's talk and the development of reasoning in the classroom. *British Educational Research Journal*, Vol. 25, no. 1, pg. 95–113.

Multiverse (2007) *TDA Initial Teacher Education Professional Resource Network*, www.multiverse.ac.uk.ac, accessed on 1 July 2007.

Parsons, M. and Stephenson, M. (2005) Developing reflective practice in student teachers: collaboration and critical partnerships. *Teachers and Teaching: Theory and Practice*, 11(1): 95–116.

Raymond, A. and Leinbach, M. (2000) Collaborative Action Research on the Learning and Teaching of Algebra: A stay of one Mathematics Teacher's Development. Education Studies in Maths, Vol. 41, no. 3, p. 283–307.

Ritchie, S.M. and Rigano, D.L. (2007) Solidarity through collaborative research, *International Journal of Qualitative Studies in Education*, 20(2), 129–50.

Sachs, J. (1999) Using teacher research as a basis for professional renewal, *Journal of In-service Education*, 25(1): 39–53.

Strauss, A. and Corbin, J. (1998) *Basics of Qualitative Research: Techniques and Procedures for Developing Grounded Theory*, 2nd edn. London: Sage Publications.

Sutherland, J. (2006) Promoting group talk and higher-order thinking in pupils by 'coaching' secondary English trainee teachers, *Literacy*, 40(2): 106–14.

Training and Development Agency (TDA) (2007) New Standards for Classroom Teachers, www.tda.gov.uk/teachers/standards, accessed November 2007.

Wells, J. (1990) Creating the conditions to encourage literature thinking, *Educational Leadership*, 47(6): 13–17.

10 Analysis of data

Sandra Eady

This chapter aims to:

- provide a brief overview of some of the main strategies and techniques for *data analysis* appropriate to the small-scale research project.
- direct you to other texts that can offer further support in the area that most suits your data analysis. Greater consideration is given to *qualitative data* as it is perhaps more appropriate for the small-scale research study; although some issues are discussed in relation to the analysis of *quantitative data*.

Qualitative data analysis

Qualitative data analysis requires 'an organisational and conceptual structure that allows the researcher to gain an overview of the data, carry out different analytical tasks and make sense of the evidence collected' (Ritchie and Lewis 2003: 217). In fact, analysing data can be one of the most challenging and time-consuming aspects of research. Even before you start your data collection, you should try to have some idea of how you might analyse your data (Opie 2004) and it is advisable to begin this process as soon as you can rather than waiting until you have collected the whole lot (Silverman 2000). Moreover, by starting this process early, it can also be illuminating and empowering as you develop an understanding of what your data is telling you in light of your original research questions (see Chapters 3 and 7).

While there is no one method of analysing qualitative data, a growing range of techniques and strategies have been identified over the last decade. Thankfully, there are now a range of texts and software that provide guidance and advice on possible strategies for data management and analysis, so that rather than being a mysterious process that can only be guessed at, the new researcher now perhaps runs the risk of being overwhelmed by techniques and strategies. A useful way of thinking about data analysis is roughly as a three-stage process (Miles and Huberman 1994; Wellington 2000; Ritchie and Lewis 2003):

- Data reduction and management, where you collate your data, summarize and sort it in relation to initial *themes, categories or codes*.
- Developing categories, concepts and *descriptive accounts* where you search across and within data sets for meanings, actions and processes.
- Generating *explanatory and analytical accounts* where you refine meanings in order to develop analytical concepts and explanations within the data and ensure its trustworthiness and credibility.

However, it has to be noted that in reality data analysis is not a linear process as this might suggest, but, in fact, there is a great deal of overlap and tracking backwards and forwards between these stages of analysis.

Computer-aided qualitative data analysis software (CAQDAS) can also be used for data management and the creation of categories, but many authors advise that for the small-scale research project it is probably not worth the time and cost involved. See Coffey and Atkinson (1998) and Opie (2004) for further discussions on this.

Data management and data reduction

This first stage of data analysis is about reducing the data so that it is manageable, allowing you to have a better understanding of issues and concepts relating to your research questions. Whatever method you decide to use for reducing and managing data, it is worth making at least one back-up copy of the *original transcripts* ensuring that each unit of text has a code or identifier so that you can trace it back to the original source. Once units of text are taken out of their original context and placed in categories, it can be hard to track them back to the data source and the original meaning of the unit of text can easily become distorted or decontextualized. Thus, a necessary part of data reduction is keeping an *audit trail* enabling you (or anyone else) to track back to the original transcripts and across data sets (see Case Studies 1 and 2).

Case Study 1

After interviewing four maths teachers about mathematics at Key Stage 3, Carole typed up each transcript and read and reread these several times, highlighting key phrases or chunks of text that seemed to be pertinent to each question asked. After a while it seemed that many of the highlighted sections related to three broad categories or concepts: 'curriculum', 'pedagogy' and 'assessment'. Carole decided to use these as initial organizing categories in order to deconstruct the teachers' perceptions of mathematics. In order to group these together in one place, she used a Word document to create a matrix for each category. For example, she pasted key phrases from each interview (followed by the page number and transcript code), which illustrated particular aspects of 'assessment', enabling her to compare comments made by the different subject leaders in relation to this category. Further analysis of these comments by noting similarities, differences and surprises allowed Carole to develop more in-depth explanatory and finally analytical accounts of assessment, distinguishing between different kinds of assessment as well as positive and negative perceptions. When developing her analytical accounts from across her data sets, Carole was able to use a pen portrait to illustrate the tensions and conflicts a teacher might face when teaching mathematics at Key Stage 3.

Reflection on Case Study 1

How you decide to divide up your text is likely to be dependent on your initial research questions, but might also reflect your reading of literature or include ideas that have emerged during the data collection or as a result of other things you have noticed or had not anticipated (see Mason 1996; Ritchie and Lewis 2003; Campbell *et al.* 2004 for more information on this). Once you have identified and highlighted themes in your data (for example, it may be that particular themes are evident in each interview conducted as well as in lessons observed), it is useful to organize and group these chunks of text together under particular categories. This will enable you to reduce the data in a systematic way and allow you to easily compare examples without having to trawl back through pages and pages of transcripts (see Ritchie and Lewis 2003: 234–6) for further guidance. Case Study 1 describes how one student reduced data in a way that enabled easy comparison across interview transcripts.

Case Study 2

> Tejpreet wanted to explore the ideas Year 1 children had about 'living things' in his science lesson when on placement. From the group interviews he conducted, he initially identified the categories of 'scientific' and 'spiritual' explanations as ones that emerged from reading the interview transcripts. In order to reduce the data, Tejpreet physically cut up the units of text from interview transcripts and sorted them into piles under these categories taking care to code each piece so that he could trace it back to the original transcript and each child. He then looked at the comments made by each child to see if they fitted these categories and noted a number of responses that did not. Rather than ignoring these he saw that he perhaps needed to develop further categories to include 'fantasy' and 'every day' explanations. This enabled him to become more sensitized to his data and, combined with his reading of literature, he began to write first explanatory and then analytical descriptions of the categories.

Developing categories and descriptive accounts

Case Study 2 describes how one student became more sensitized to his data. This is an important stage and as you search for meanings, you may find it necessary to refine your categories and concepts, possibly developing new ones and merging others. One way to help you do this is to focus on actions and processes or note any instances of conflict or contradiction within your data. Alternatively, you may look at how interviewees use key words in context or if there are repetitions of words and phrases across data sets. Another approach might be to look for surprises or negative cases, methods of social control, how people manage social relationships, acquire and maintain status or solve problems to further interrogate the data. In fact, there are many different strategies and techniques to help you in this process and it is up to you to decide which are most appropriate for your analysis.

Ritchie and Lewis (2003) and Campbell *et al.* (2004) provide comprehensive accounts of categorizing and coding data by moving from the initial descriptions to a summary of key elements and more abstract concepts. While the online qualitative data analysis (QDA) website outline some of the more common strategies of analysis, Roberts-Holmes (2005) uses a specific example from students' early years research project to illustrate how themes can be generated and interpreted in relation to literature.

Generating explanatory and analytical accounts

While it is important to 'sort' and 're-sort' your data as described above, it is also important not to try and make the data fit the categories, but to modify the categories by returning to the original transcripts. As you read through the data in this way and combine this with your previous reading of literature, you will be able to refine your descriptive accounts of categories to more explanatory and analytical ones.

There are different ways explanations can be developed from your analysis. For example, you may describe a range of explanations given by participants; use a powerful analytical concept that has arisen from your data; or use explanations from other studies to provide a way of explaining your findings. For a more in-depth discussion see Mason (1996: 135–8) or Ritchie and Lewis (2003: 253–5). It is important that you are not only systematic and rigorous in your analysis but that you can demonstrate this to others in the way you justify issues of *reliability* and *validity* (see Chapter 6). Mason (1996) provides a good discussion around this while Silverman (2000) also considers five interrelated ways of thinking critically about qualitative data analysis.

Quantitative data analysis

Denscombe (2003) argues that while it is acceptable for the small-scale research project to use quantitative data, many reflect a limited understanding of *descriptive statistics* and what forms of data presentation are appropriate (see also Chapter 6). Opie (2004) also provides a frank account of when quantitative data analysis is justified and what level of sophistication is needed for 'Masters'-level study. Both Denscombe (2003) and Opie (2004) provide useful chapters on the presentation of quantitative data giving practical advice on the compilation of tables and charts. Campbell *et al.* (2004) provide you with a step-by-step description of the five main kinds of question used in questionnaire surveys, showing how these can be structured and coded in preparation for analysis. They also explain how the data can be organized and entered into an Excel spreadsheet. Muijs (2004) also provides a very accessible starting point for students who have no experience of quantitative analysis and explains how to enter data into a Statistical Package for the Social Sciences (SPSS).

Glossary

audit trail   providing evidence of how you got from the raw data to your knowledge claims by indexing.

data analysis   different techniques used to interrogate, interpret and develop an understanding of your raw data.
descriptive accounts   describing what the data shows.
descriptive statistics   using charts, graphs or text to describe the data numerically.

explanatory and analytical accounts   explaining and theorizing from the data.

original transcripts   typed or written accounts of social interaction, for example, observations and interviews.

qualitative data   non-numerical data that seeks to develop under-standings and explanations of social interaction, for example through observation, interviews, diaries and children's work. It tends to produce and analyse in-depth and detailed data.
quantitative data   usually numerical data that seeks to describe patterns and trends in phenomena. This is normally derived from questionnaires, statistical surveys or experiments. Analysis of quantita-tive data tends to provide overall patterns and generalizations.

reliability   in terms of analysis of qualitative data, this is seen as the way in which chunks of texts or phrases are consistently grouped in the same themes or categories by different observers (Hammersley 1992: 67) *What's Wrong with Ethnography: Methodological Explorations*. London: Routledge.

themes, categories or codes   ways of grouping and organizing your data under units of meaning to enable a deeper analysis and under-standing.

validity   in qualitative approaches, several methods of data collection or analysis may be used in order to provide an accurate account of events or actions. In quantitative approaches, validity and reliability is concerned with the research process and findings being replicated or copied by someone else.

Where you can find further support for data analysis

Campbell, A., McNamara, O. and Gilroy, P. (2004) *Practitioner Research and Professional Development in Education*. London: Paul Chapman Publishing. This provides an accessible account of both qualitative and quantitative data analysis that is appropriate for small-scale research projects. Although aimed at serving practitioners, the techniques and strategies outlined for data analysis are entirely appropriate for trainee teachers working on small-scale research projects at 'M' level.

Coffey, A. and Atkinson, P. (1998) *Making Sense of Qualitative Data*. London: Sage Publishing. Chapter 2 explains how to link concepts to data and provides an account of the coding process. Chapter 4 looks at the use of metaphors while Chapter 6 explains analysing and theorizing. Chapter 7 considers CAQDAS.

Denscombe, M. (2003) *The Good Research Guide*, 2nd edn. Maidenhead: Open University Press. These are useful but adopt a much wider social science perspective and do not address the particular needs of trainee teachers.

Lincoln, Y.S. and Guba, E.G. (1985) *Naturalistic Inquiry*. London: Sage Publications. Chapter 12 discusses the techniques of data processing particularly the 'constant comparison method'. Appendix A provides a useful overview of an audit trail.

Mason, J. (1996) *Qualitative Researching*. London: Sage Publishing. Chapters 6 and 7 give an informative and thought-provoking account of categorizing data and producing analyses and explanations.

Miles, M.B. and Huberman, A.M. (1994) *Qualitative Data Analysis*, 2nd edn. London: Sage Publications. An extremely detailed and well-written account of qualitative data analysis. Probably better suited for Masters dissertations or Doctoral theses.

Muijs, D. (2004) *Doing Quantitative Research in Education*. London: Sage Publications. Provides an introduction to quantitative data analysis and SPSS for students who have little or no prior knowledge of quantitative methods.

Gibbs, G., Fielding, N., Lewins, A. and Taylor, C., *On line QDA*, www.onlineqda.hud.ac.uk, accessed 2 July 2007. This is a good web-based resource for QDA, funded by the Economic and Social Research Council (ESRC). There is a wealth of advice and examples of QDA that includes an explanation of themes and coding including descriptive coding and analytical/theoretical coding. There is also a section on choosing and using CAQDAS, including a helpful summary of what qualitative software can and cannot do. Although not specifically focused on educational research, it does give a thorough explanation of data analysis for beginning researchers.

Opie, C. (ed.) (2004) *Doing Educational Research: A Guide to First-time Researchers*. London: Sage Publications. Chapter 7 gives a very good account of presenting data, particularly tables and charts while Chapters 8 and 9 provide accounts of using CAQDAS.

Ritchie, J. and Lewis, J. (eds) (2003) *Qualitative Research Practice*. London: Sage Publications. Chapter 8 deals with the traditions and approaches to qualitative analysis and discusses computer-assisted qualitative methods and gives an analytic hierarchy. Chapter 9 outlines three main aspects of qualitative data analysis and discusses ways to tackle analysis of group data.

Roberts-Holmes, G. (2005) *Doing Your Early Years Research Project*. London: Paul Chapman. Chapter 10 illustrates, through the example of a student research project, how to understand and sort data by generating categories and themes.

Robson, C. (2002) *Real World Research: A Resource for Social Scientists and Practitioner Researchers*, 2nd edn. Oxford: Blackwell. Provides comprehensive and detailed information on most aspects of data collection and analysis. In particular Part IV, Chapters 11–12, provides strategies for analysing quantitative and qualitative data.

Silverman, D. (2000) *Doing Qualitative Research: A Practical Handbook*. London: Sage Publications. In particular, Part Three specifically focuses on analysing data. Chapter 12 discusses the pros and cons of using computers and evaluates specific CAQDAS. Chapter 13 is particularly illuminating in the way it addresses issues of validity and reliability within the process of qualitative data analysis.

Strauss, A. and Corbin, J. (1998) *Basics of Qualitative Research*, 2nd edn. London: Sage Publications. Provides a substantial and detailed account of grounded theory and its origins, again possibly better suited to higher-level study.

Wellington, J. (2000) *Educational Research, Contemporary Issues and Practical Approaches*. London: Continuum. Part 3, Chapter 10 deals with qualitative data and provides a useful overview of the stages/processes of data analysis.

Part IV Writing it up and making it public

11 Presenting research in writing

Sue Pope

In this chapter you are:

- introduced to the essential ingredients of any written report, ensuring you meet the academic criteria by understanding what is required;
- offered strategies for managing the writing process leading to timely completion of your report;
- given advice on how to adapt your report for different audiences, for example a professional journal aimed at teachers or a research journal aimed at educational researchers.

Lawrence Stenhouse was a great advocate of the teacher as researcher. He described research as 'systematic enquiry made public' (1985: 9) and wrote 'Publication has two functions. It opens work to criticism and consequently to refinement; and it also disseminates the fruits of research and makes possible the cumulation of knowledge' (Stenhouse 1985: 17). There are many ways of making research public but the most common is a written report. Your institution will have guidelines on what is required, both in terms of word length and structure and the academic criteria you will be expected to meet. The National Qualifications Framework (www.qca.org.uk/qca_5967.aspx) means that while the interpretation of standards and precise expectations may vary from institution to institution, the standards expected for work at a given level (for example Masters/Postgraduate/Undergraduate) are the same across the country. These standards are monitored through the system of external examiners where experienced colleagues from other institutions act as critical friends, scrutinizing samples of work and ensuring that standards are consistently upheld and students are treated fairly.

What needs to be included?

The purpose of writing up your research is to share your findings with others, thereby contributing to what is known about the area you chose to investigate. To give your work credibility you need to convince the reader that you are knowledgeable about what is already known and can locate your work within that body of knowledge. You also need to demonstrate an understanding of how research can be undertaken and an awareness of the limitations of your chosen methodology. In discussing your findings you need to demonstrate an understanding of how these relate to what is already known. Finally, you need to draw conclusions about your research question that are based on the evidence you have collected and identify possibilities and opportunities for further research.

The voice you adopt in your report is important. You cannot assume that your reader is an expert in the field, so you need to avoid jargon and ensure that any specialist terminology is defined. It is perfectly OK to write in the first person for a piece of small-scale research, unless you are advised explicitly not to do so. You need to take care to be consistent with tense. The past tense is the safest to use. Any shorthand needs to be given in full the first time it is used (for example Training and Development Agency for Schools (TDA)) and things need to be given their correct name (for example do not refer to SATs but End of Key Stage National Tests).

You need to be pedantic throughout to reference your sources accurately and in a consistent style. Most institutions and journals use *Harvard Referencing* for social sciences, which includes education (see Chapter 3). It is important that you follow the guidelines provided. If you do not give references for ideas from other sources, you may be accused of plagiarism, which can have very serious consequences for your academic career. This can be avoided by keeping notes on all your reading with the source written in the correct style (see Chapters 3 and 4). There are bibliographical packages, such as EndNote or BibTex, which allow you to record all your readings in a consistent way and makes referencing them in your writing easy.

You are strongly advised to build in time to review drafts of your report. Asking a friend to read your report looking at clarity of argument and quality of written English is a valuable strategy.

Abstract/synopsis

The very first thing your reader will encounter is the *abstract or synopsis*. Written at the very end of the writing process, this summarizes in one (short) paragraph what your research is about. The abstract needs to inform the potential reader whether or not this is a relevant piece of work for them to read. You will have read several abstracts as you read research papers in preparation for your research. You may want to consider what sort of abstract was most helpful.

The abstract needs to be succinct and factually accurate. It should identify clearly your research question, the methodology used and key findings. That level of detail should help the potential reader decide whether or not your report is relevant to them. For an assessed piece of work your abstract informs the reader of your ability to summarize the key features of your research.

Contents

This needs to be accurate and is the navigation tool for your report. Some software will allow you to develop a contents page dynamically. This can be very helpful as it allows you to cut and paste without having to continually update the contents. On the other hand if your report is fairly short, then the contents page can be compiled at the end.

Introduction

Your introduction needs to provide the contextual detail behind your research and the development of your research question. It should clarify why you have undertaken your research, its personal relevance and its wider educational significance. You need to introduce the structure of your report making explicit reference to the rest of your report; for example, the literature review, the methodology, findings and discussion. You need to ensure that the research question(s) is expressed clearly and that any ambiguity of meaning is clarified. The introduction should act as an 'appetizer' to the rest of your report. While your research proposal will provide the basis of your introduction, it is likely to need refining and reworking as you progress. The introduction, like the abstract, needs to be completed towards the end of the writing process as you need to ensure it is consistent with the rest of your report.

In developing your research focus and research question(s), you may undertake quite a bit of reflective writing (see Chapters 2, 3 and 7). This will provide a valuable starting point for writing part of the introduction but it is unlikely to be used verbatim. Your report is a formal document and while an account of your personal journey identifying your research focus is appropriate, it needs to be edited identifying key points and significant moments rather than giving every detail.

The literature review

The *literature review* is based on the reading you have undertaken to become an expert in your area of research. It should not simply be a summary of each book or article you have read. Rather, you need to identify key themes that are relevant to your research. You need to compare and contrast different authors and researchers, demonstrating a good awareness of current opinion, theory and knowledge that is relevant to your research.

You are expected to adopt a critical approach to your reading and to engage with both research and theory (see Chapter 4). It is reasonable not to refer to everything you have read in the literature because you feel it is not relevant. However, avoid leaving something out because it appears to contradict the rest of the literature you have surveyed. An awareness of contradictions and controversies around your area of interest is likely to strengthen your report and the quality of discussion about your findings.

Your literature review is not expected to include a critical account of the methods used in the research you have read as that should feature in the next section of your report.

Methodology

This section of your report allows you to demonstrate an awareness and understanding of social science research methodology appropriate to your research. You need to identify the paradigm (for example practitioner research) within which you are working, its benefits and potential pitfalls and to consider whether or not alternatives might be appropriate (see Chapters 6 and 7).

You need to show due consideration of the range of possible methods that might be suitable for your study. When critiquing methodologies you need to refer to literature. You need to justify your chosen approach based on its appropriateness, what other researchers have done in the field and what will be feasible in the time available, giving due regard to validity, reliability, triangulation and ethical considerations. It is well worth developing an ethical plan and including this in your appendix (see Chapter 5).

If using a questionnaire or interview schedule, the choice of questions need to be linked to the literature review explaining why they are appropriate to your research question. Depending on how much time you have for your study, it is well worth piloting your research instruments; the outcomes of the pilot can be reported in the appendix and alluded to in the methodology section.

For this section of your report you need to demonstrate knowledge and understanding of the research *methodology* literature and a critical approach to the research methodology adopted by the researchers whose work you included in the literature review. Please note that there are no right answers when it comes to research methods; it is invariably a balance between pragmatism (you only have so much time and resource to complete the research) and ideology (the data needs to be valid and reliable). Whatever methods you adopt you need to show that you have conformed to institutional ethical guidelines and treated participants with appropriate sensitivity (see Chapter 5).

The findings

You need to give a brief account of what actually happened in practice. To what extent did your planned research actually happen? You then need to present the outcomes. Raw data rarely features in the report itself, although you may decide to include samples of data in the appendices from which you select examples to discuss. Including a full interview transcript in an appendix allows the reader to make a judgement about your choice of examples. You need to summarize the data. To what extent can you be confident about the validity and reliability (see Chapter 6)? To what extent does one data source corroborate another? If there are contradictions, why do you think these have occurred (see Chapter 10)?

If you have undertaken a small-scale piece of research it is unlikely that quantitative methodology is appropriate. It is easy to generate a bar chart or pie chart using Excel, or to calculate some statistics even though your data set is tiny or your data are not suitable for such analysis. Do take care not to include such analysis unless it is appropriate and offers additional insight into the data.

You need to have immersed yourself in the data in order to identify key themes (see Chapter 10). You can then discuss your data and justify your choice of themes, making links to literature where appropriate. It is essential that you refer to your original research questions when summarizing your findings.

Conclusion

Together with your introduction, the conclusion should provide the 'bread and butter' of your report. When you read the introduction and the conclusion, are they consistent and coherent? Does the way they have been written signpost the rest of the report? You need to make explicit reference to your research question and the extent to which your findings allow you to answer it. Your conclusions need to be firmly grounded in the evidence that you have managed to collect. You should make links to your literature review and other sections of your report as appropriate to help the reader understand why you have come to your conclusions.

You need to identify any limitations to your study and the generalizability of your findings. However, resist the temptation to be overly modest, that is do not denigrate your findings when discussing limitations; rather restrict your comments to the limitations of the research in terms of resources, time, sample, and so on. So discussing limitations does not mean highlighting 'flaws' in your research – your audience will not expect to read that your methodology or literature review, and so on should have been done completely differently, otherwise they will naturally ask, 'Why did you do it that way?' You should also identify areas that would be worthy of further study.

It is always worth including some personal reflection identifying how your research will impact on your professional practice in future (see Chapter 3).

Bibliography

All the literature that you have explicitly referenced in your report needs to be listed in alphabetical order consistent with your institution's expectations. If in doubt use the Harvard system of referencing (see Chapter 4). It is very important that you check your bibliography is complete and accurate. Software like Endnote or Bibtex can be extremely valuable in helping ensure consistency between your bibliography and the references in your report.

Appendices

Judicious use of *appendices* allows you to keep to the word count while incorporating greater detail where necessary and more substantial examples of data. Anything that is included in the appendix needs to be referenced to literature where appropriate. Items in an appendix will not be looked at by the reader unless you make explicit reference to them in the main body of your report. You need to ensure that the report is coherent if read without looking at items in appendices, and that what is there enhances the report by enriching the data available to the reader and providing additional background information.

How you will be assessed

Your institution will provide assessment criteria based on national expectations for your level of study, the learning outcomes for the module you are presenting the assignment for and agreed generic criteria that are used across your institution. It is essential that you have read and fully understood the assessment criteria. Your tutor will be able to advise you on precisely what is required and how best to present your research so you fully meet the requirements.

The Quality Assurance Agency for Higher Education set out the generic expectations for Masters level study. You are expected to be working at the forefront of knowledge in your field. Using up-to-date literature and ensuring that your chosen approach is justified and informed by what has been done before can show this. You are expected to have an understanding of how research advances the boundaries of knowledge. Again, this is related to your understanding of previous research in your chosen area but also to the strengths and limitations of different research methodologies. You are expected to show originality when tackling complex issues systematically and creatively.

Someone who achieves a Masters qualification is expected to have developed the skills that ensure they exercise sound judgement, take personal responsibility and show initiative when working in a complex and unpredictable professional environment.

Adapting your report for different audiences

There are a range of ways in which you might choose to publish your research. Your own background reading will acquaint you with the range of publications that you may wish to consider submitting an article to. Most publications have a target audience from practitioners (for example *Junior Education, Mathematics Teaching, Primary Science Review,* and so on) to researchers (for example *British Education Research Journal, Educational Researcher,* and so on). There are also conference papers that can take the form of a poster presentation to a full paper.

Any publication will have a set of guidelines on precisely how to submit an article. This may include a template, which must be used if you want the editors to give your proposed article serious consideration. You need to be clear about the nature of the target audience as this will help you to tailor your account appropriately.

An article that is aimed at practitioners will contain only a very brief summary of the background literature and the research methodology. What is needed is a clear statement of your findings, how they were arrived at, any limitations and implications for practice. On the other hand, a research paper, while not being as full as the report prepared for assessment does need to show a good understanding of the relevant literature, including a justification for the research methodology adopted. The outcomes of your research need to be discussed systematically and analytically making links with background reading. Your conclusion needs to be clear, identifying limitations and potential for further study.

The decision about publication is the responsibility of the editors. The editors will contact you indicating whether or not they are likely to publish; typically, they will invite you to make some modifications, for example remove material that they consider unnecessary or expand/ rewrite a part to improve clarity. For research journals your article is likely to be sent to two or three independent reviewers who are experts in your field of research. Their views will inform the decision of the editors.

Presenting your work at a conference may well require you to write an accompanying paper. Depending on the target audience for the conference and the planned format for the proceedings, this could be anything from a paragraph that is likely to be based on your abstract to a paper aimed at researchers. A poster presentation means that you identify key features of your research and present them as an A3 or A2 poster. During the conference, participants will have the opportunity to look at your poster and ask you questions about your work.

You are strongly advised to ask a friend, colleague or tutor to look critically at your work before you submit it for publication.

Planning to meet the deadlines

It is never too soon to begin writing up your work (see Chapters 3 and 10). As you read it is worth recording the articles and books you have read using the expected format for your bibliography and keeping brief notes of key points. As you begin to synthesize ideas and formulate your research strategy, it is worth keeping notes as these will form a valuable resource for your final report.

Be realistic when estimating the time needed to write your report. It will take much longer than you expect! You need to aim for a first draft at least a fortnight before the deadline in order that you can get feedback from your critical reader and act on it. Breaking the report into sections and setting deadlines for each of them can help to make the writing process less onerous and give you a sense of achievement that helps to keep you motivated.

The background reading and the research methodology can be written up before the research is completed. You may find that you will need to revise your writing to ensure consistency and coherence once you have completed your report. This is an inevitable consequence of writing an extended report section by section.

Some people find a written plan with target dates is helpful in managing the writing process (see Table 11.1). By adding completion dates it can inform necessary adjustments to the plan so the deadline is met.

Table 11.1: Written plan

What needs to be done	Target date	Completion date
Formulate research question		
Undertake background reading		
Draft review of literature		
Draft research methodology section		
Draft the introduction		
Write up outcomes		
Analyse results		
Draft conclusions		
Review the introduction		
Draft the abstract		
Review and refine report		
Pass report to critical friend		
Make adjustments		
Print report		
Deadline		

Conclusion

The essential ingredients of any piece of writing about your research are:

- a clear statement of purpose;
- an understanding of background literature relevant to your field of study;
- an understanding of the effectiveness of different research methodologies;
- a justification of your chosen research methodology;
- a clear presentation of research findings and analysis of outcomes;
- a clear conclusion identifying limitations and potential for further study.

You need to understand the requirements for your writing, for example the assessment guidance and criteria, or the guidelines for your chosen publication. You also need to plan to complete your writing in good time for any deadline. Difficulties with printing are never accepted as an excuse for late submission. Use friends, tutors and/or colleagues to critique your work prior to submission.

Bibliography

Bell, J. (2005) *Doing Your Research Project*, 4th edn. Maidenhead: Open University Press.

Hyatt, D. (2004) *Writing Research*, in C. Opie (ed.) *Doing Educational Research*. London: Sage Publications.

Macintyre, C. (2000) *The Art of Action Research in the Classroom*. London: David Fulton.

McNiff, J., Lomax, P. and Whitehead, J. (2003) *You and Your Action Research Project*, 2nd edn. London: Routledge Falmer.

Stenhouse, L. (1985) What counts as research?, in J. Rudduck and D. Hopkins (eds) *Research as a Basis for Teaching: Readings from the Work of Lawrence Stenhouse*. London: Heinemann.

Turk, C. and Kirkman, J. (2001) *Effective Writing*. London: E&FN Spon, www.qaa.ac.uk, accessed June 2007.

Glossary

abstract / synopsis   a brief summary of your research that helps the reader to decide whether or not your report is of interest to them.

appendices   use to add additional detail or data. Ensure that the report is consistent without them and that they are referenced explicitly from the main body of the report.

Harvard referencing   system of referencing that is commonly used for social sciences including education.

literature review   a synthesis of the reading of theory and research relevant to your study in which you identify key themes, resonances and controversies.

methodology   understanding the range of methods available and their inherent strengths and weaknesses is important when justifying the approach taken in a research study.

12 Presenting research in a range of forums

Sandra Eady

The aim of this chapter is to:

- help you consider why your research project might be of interest to a wider audience other than your college tutors and what other *forums* might be appropriate;
- offer you guidance about the technicalities and some strategies for presenting your research findings to others.

Why you should make your research findings public

Although up to now the focus has been to produce a small-scale research project that can be assessed by your tutor, it might be that the research findings are of interest to a wider audience and could be presented in other forums. It is very likely that the focus of your research project has been on a particular educational issue that is highly topical. Therefore, it is important that you realize the value of having a voice in public and professional debate. By presenting your small-scale research in other forums beyond your assessed assignment, you will have the opportunity to engage in *professional dialogue*, and reflect critically on the findings and wider implications of your research. Moreover, *disseminating* your findings more widely will enable you to:

- prepare and practise for talking publicly;
- share findings so that others may reflect upon them in relation to their own contexts;
- open up debate to others from similar or different perspectives.

Campbell *et al.* (2004) suggest that it is only within the last 10 or so years that educational research and, in particular, *practitioner research* has been more widely reported. By putting your research in the public arena and sharing findings allows others to consider and discuss the implications that may in turn help to inform and shape practice at classroom and school level, and even beyond (see Chapters 1 and 2).

Who else might be interested in your research?

Internal seminars and conferences

Your course might give you a chance to share your project with fellow students or colleagues through a university *seminar programme* or an *internal conference*. This is a great opportunity to share your research and engage in further debate around your research findings and outcomes. You may find that other students have conducted similar research to you but in a different setting or approached it in a different way. This could also help develop further questions and possible areas of research.

Case Study 1

John was on placement in a primary school where a number of pupils had English as an additional language. He was interested in why some pupils made very good progress while others seemed to struggle. Working closely with the bilingual teacher, he discovered that those pupils who had poor literacy skills in their mother tongue were beginning to exhibit similar difficulties in English. While he was able to gain a deeper understanding of the development of literacy through his research, he was also able to share this with fellow students during a college seminar programme.

Professional settings

If you have carried out research in a professional setting such as a school or subject department, then it is worth suggesting that you would be willing to give some feedback at a *staff or departmental meeting*. You might even produce a summary sheet of the main findings and conclusions from your research. Before giving presentations in professional contexts, it is advisable to talk to your supervisor to ensure that what you say is credible, ethically sensitive and insightful in the way you can show how your research can build on current practice within the school or professional setting (see Chapters 5 and 6 concerning ethical issues, validity and reliability). Remember that the practitioners within the school have a thorough knowledge and understanding of the context in which they work and the day-to-day realities they face.

Case Study 2

The science department in which Beth was on placement in a large secondary school had recently introduced mind-mapping as a tool for developing conceptual understanding in science in Key Stage 3 classes. Beth thought that she would like to focus on the different ways that she could use mind-mapping as a tool in her science lessons. The head of science was very interested in her findings and asked her if she would be willing to present these at a departmental meeting after school. The discussion resulting from the presentation enabled a wider understanding of the potential value of mind-maps used individually, as a stimulus for group discussion as well as a formative assessment tool.

Professional magazines

Other ways of making your research public could be through publication in professional magazines. You would need to write to the *editor* providing an overview of your research. They are often looking for current topical material that would be of interest to their readers and are likely to advise you on how you might structure your article in order to suit the readership of the magazine. Writing for a *professional journal* would probably mean that you would select and summarize bits of your research project in order to suit the audience.

It is also worth looking through the magazine that you have in mind to see how other articles have been written and presented. Examples of such magazines for Early Years and Primary Education might include *Nursery World, Nursery Education, Child Education, Junior Education, Primary Maths and Science, Primary History, Primary Music, Primary Science Review.* Professional publications aimed at Secondary Education include *Mathematics in School, Secondary English, Teaching Geography, Teaching*

History and *School Science Review*. There are also cross-phase publications such as *Teaching Citizenship, RE Today, Teaching and Learning, Viewpoint* (learning disability) or *Learning Disability Practice*.

Case Study 3

Rachel had been looking at fairy-tales and nursery rhymes as starting points for science investigations. From her analysis of the small-scale research project, it was clear that the findings would be of value to others, particularly parents of nursery-aged children. As a result of a discussion with her college tutor and appropriate guidance, she wrote a short article that summarized the findings and emphasized the opportunities for developing contexts for science within the home and school and submitted it to an Early Years professional magazine, which was subsequently accepted and published with minor modifications.

Peer-reviewed journals

In order to reach a wider national or international audience, you may consider submitting your research to a *peer-reviewed journal* (see Chapter 11). Once received, the editor will send your research article out for peer review and you will receive back detailed comments as to whether your research is of sufficient quality and interest to be published in the journal. Before considering a peer-reviewed journal, it is worth consulting with your tutor which journal might be appropriate and what changes or modifications you will need to make before submitting. For example, if you are considering an international journal you may have to include some background information, explain terminology or practice, as terms such as 'Key Stage 3' or 'Primary Strategy' have little meaning outside of the UK.

National conferences

Another forum for disseminating your research might be at a *national education conference*. Here you are able to make your research public to a wider audience, which may include other teachers, subject leaders, head teachers or even representatives from local authorities, government agencies and education lecturers and researchers. Many subject or professional associations host conferences in different parts of the UK, usually on an annual basis. Once you have decided on an appropriate conference, submit an overview of your research (usually an abstract) often between 200 and 500 words to the conference organizers who will tell you if they are able to offer you a slot for presenting your research.

Alternatively, many conferences offer opportunities for *poster presentations*. Here you prepare a poster on a large board that summarizes your research, possibly using pictures and diagrams. The information again needs to be a summary of your research including the initial question, brief outline of data methods, findings and implications. This needs to be displayed in a visual and attractive way so that it is easy to read and understand. In many instances you will be standing by your poster and should be able to provide additional information or more detail to interested observers who want to know more about your research. You might also make available a short handout.

Examples of such conferences might include the Association for Science Education (ASE), the National Association of Primary Education (NAPE), the Association of the Study of Primary Education (ASPE), the Mathematical Association, the Geography Association, the English Association and the PSHE Subject Association, but there are many more.

Preparing your research for wider dissemination

While a wider audience may not want to know about the intricacies of how you went about the research or how many observations and interviews you did, they may be interested in the reliability and validity of the evidence on which you base your conclusions and recommendations (see Chapter 6). Campbell *et al.* (2004) recommend that you are honest and upfront about your doubts and inconsistencies, and modest about your successes (see also Chapter 11). They also stress that your research must be accessible in terms of the language it is written in and where it is published, so that teachers are able to and will want to access and read it. It is advisable to talk this through with your college supervisor. Always make sure that any claims you are likely to make are supported with adequate and convincing evidence from your data. If in doubt, only present claims that you feel comfortable with. This is especially important if the findings you present are counter to what was expected or anticipated, or are likely to be somewhat controversial. Remember that generalizations from small-scale research need to be treated with extreme caution. Similarly, your interpretation of the research may not represent another person's interpretation.

Revisiting ethical issues

Whatever alternative forum for presenting your research, it is important that you reconsider ethical issues as well as the quality of evidence you use to support statements made (see Chapter 5). While participants may have been happy to divulge information about themselves or their institution or professional setting for your research assignment, they may not be happy for it to be in the public domain. Similarly, while some of your controversial findings do not appear emotive or controversial to you or your tutors, you may feel uncomfortable presenting them to the participants of the participating school. Therefore, it is important to get permission again from participant(s) or the school for wider dissemination or to ensure that participants and institutions understand and are in agreement with your intentions to open your research up to a wider audience. In other words, you will need to reconsider issues of individual or institutional sensitivity and openly consult and negotiate modifications that might be necessary in order to prevent damage to people or educational settings and gain consent for wider dissemination. If in doubt consult your tutors or get advice from ethics experts in your university.

Skills and strategies for an oral presentation of your research

Whether you are giving an oral presentation at a staff or governor's meeting, or at an internal or external conference, there are a few basic rules that may help your presentation go smoothly. Whether you decide to use overhead transparencies or a PowerPoint presentation, the key points below all apply.

Before the presentation

- Find out the length of time allocated and organize your presentation so that there is time for questions at the end.
- Find out who your audience is likely to be and modify your presentation to suit your audience.
- Do not produce too many slides and allow yourself about two minutes to explain them (5 slides for a 10-minute talk).
- Have no more than five key points on each slide – DO NOT READ STRAIGHT FROM THE SLIDES.
- Run through your presentation so that you are sure that you can keep to the time-scale allocated.

During the presentation

- Arrive early and check you know where the room is and that all the resources and equipment you need are ready and working.
- Arrange furniture and chairs in a way that you are comfortable with.
- Although you are likely to feel nervous, try to pace yourself and not speak too quickly, vary the tone of your voice and leave pauses as you move from one point to the next.
- Do not use clichés, worn out phrases or jargon.
- Use language markers such as 'and now . . .' 'the next point . . .'.
- Always start by introducing yourself, the topic and outline your aims for the presentation. Depending on the audience, you may like to provide a brief context to the research and how it relates to the wider picture and why it was done.
- Then outline how you conducted the research and any limitations to the approach you took.
- Explain clearly and concisely your findings.
- Take account of any weaknesses/limitations in your evidence, and outline implications for practice.
- Your presentation should finish by summing up with clear conclusions and, if appropriate, invite questions.

Handling questions

When presenting to a wider audience, you are likely to be giving an oral report and will need to be prepared to respond to questions from the audience. While you do not know exactly what you will be asked, you can perhaps anticipate some possible questions and think about how you might respond to them. The points below are also worth considering.

- Decide if you want questions during or at the end of your presentation. The latter enables you to keep the flow of your presentation and stops you from getting sidetracked.
- Try to avoid taking questions from just one person and address your responses to the whole audience.
- Be honest if you do not know the answer to a question.
- Be polite if someone tries to put you down or disagrees with your interpretation; do not enter into an argument.
- If there are no questions, you might like to have one prepared to ask the audience to consider or debate.

Glossary

disseminating sharing ideas, opinions and research.

editor a person who selects material for publication.

forum a place or meeting for public discussion.

internal conference an organized meeting within an institution that provides opportunities for individuals to share their research with others.

national education conference an organized meeting for a wide range of individuals to share and discuss their research based on a particular theme.

peer-reviewed journal a themed magazine that sends articles (many based on original research) out to experts to decide if the article is of sufficient quality to be published.
poster presentations a summary of the research (main question/focus, methods and findings) displayed on a large (A2) poster for others to see and comment on.
practitioner research research conducted into one's own practice.
professional dialogue discussion or debate about aspects relating to educational issues.
professional journal a magazine that publishes educational articles of interest, often relating to a particular theme and readership.

seminar programme a small discussion group that meets regularly over a period of time to discuss educational issues and research.
staff or departmental meeting a regular meeting held usually after school in which issues that relate to the school are discussed by its staff.

Reference

Campbell, A., McNamara, O. and Gilroy, P. (2004) *Practitioner Research and Professional Development in Education*. London: Paul Chapman.

13 Next steps

Helen Scott

The objectives of this chapter are:

- to discuss the role of teacher researcher as part of the professional identity of a teacher;
- to explore the challenges and opportunities of being a beginning teacher as well as a beginning researcher, in terms of what it is possible to achieve;
- to consider the reasons for continuing study and research and the various means of achieving this.

This chapter aims to explore your role as a teacher who may engage in research activity alongside initial training, the induction year and beyond, and to encourage you to continue research and study in the future. As a beginner in research, you will experience the practical difficulties and potential rewards of managing research alongside your planning, teaching, assessing and other myriad activities comprising the work of a teacher in the twenty-first century. This chapter will support you in considering, beginning and sustaining research activity. The research process is presented as complex and *multidimensional*, while acknowledging that choices are informed by a mixture of personal, professional and practical factors, that is the things you have some control over, those you have no control over and the ways you choose to deal with them. The chapter concludes with two case studies that show very different approaches to researching practice.

The role of teacher researcher as part of the professional identity of a teacher

You will already have ideas about your professional role and identity; these probably include passionate enthusiasm for your subject, enjoying working with young people and wishing to give them opportunities to enjoy different subjects and make the most of their potential. The current version of the Professional Standards for Teachers (DfES 2007) have given *'professionalism'* significant importance, relating it to understanding the legal responsibilities teachers have, communicating effectively with parents, working collaboratively with colleagues, being self-critical and innovative, identifying and taking responsibility for your own professional development, to name a few areas. To promote the notion, explored in earlier chapters, that undertaking research will help you to develop your knowledge and understanding of teaching and learning while training and beyond, research can also be said to have the potential to contribute significantly to your professional role and identity.

One of the 'problems' or criticisms of educational research (Carr 2003) is that it is not generalizable to all settings, as other research might be, because it relates to specific contexts; if we take this view then it could be said that:

> *only* field professionals could be in a position to appreciate the precise nature of their own or their pupils' practical needs in this or that particular context and so only such professionals could be well placed to research teaching.
>
> (Carr 2003: 24).

Hammersley (2002: 4), in the same vein, explores Stenhouse's argument 'that effective curricular improvements could only come about through being developed and tested in the classroom by teachers; indeed that this was the core of a proper understanding of teacher professionalism'.

Carr (2003) explores the relationship between theory and practice in relation to professional identity in some depth, examining competing perspectives. Having considered different arguments, he concludes that although teachers do not necessarily need theories to be great teachers, what they definitely do need is the ability to make judgements about theories put forward to them to consider in relation to their practice, and engaging with theory develops capacity 'for an educated professional appreciation of the large questions about justice ... in which education is morally implicated' (Carr 2003: 63–4).

The worth of research is not necessarily related to the occupation of those who produced it; there is value in understanding education from different perspectives. Your specific perspectives as a student, beginning or more experienced teacher may be of particular value and interest to a school; you will be both a (more or less developed) 'insider' to the profession of teaching, but come with certain perspectives arising from being an 'outsider', if you are new to teaching, or have worked in other schools.

The particular challenges and opportunities of being a beginning teacher as well as a beginning researcher

The challenge of choosing an area of research has been discussed earlier in Chapters 2, 3 and 7; it is also worth exploring certain issues in relation to your position as a beginning teacher. You may feel it is a simple case of choosing what you are interested in, within your teaching. This might include an issue in your subject area or an organizational difficulty, for example related to managing the classroom environment, or, more broadly, an issue within the school's development plan. The particular trouble you will face as a beginning teacher is how to choose a *small* focus, as you will be learning so much (though this is also a problem for more experienced teachers as your work involves so many concerns and activities). Although your research will take place alongside your planning, teaching, and so on, it will be helpful to conceive all your activity as elements that will facilitate each other: 'Education is not just a matter of what you teach; crucially it is concerned with how you teach. Critical pedagogy requires that you continue to reflect on both these questions but in addition ask the question why?' (Addison and Burgess 2000: 2). Your research may well become the means by which you deeply reflect on your own practice and ask 'why?'.

It is important that your choice of focus *matters* to you; you will expend much time and thinking on it. Hopefully, what matters does so because it affects your pupils' learning and experiences of school. Your research has the potential to make improvements for your pupils, even if on a small scale in particular areas (see Chapters 1 and 8). The notion of 'action research' making improvements for children's educational experiences and achievement is explored in a range of literature (for example Elliot 1991; Altrichter *et al.* 1993; Dadds 1995 and Somekh 2006; Somekh and Lewin 2005.

A further consideration of your personal reasons for choosing a research area, or even to research at all, is to feel you have some *agency*. Somekh explores the idea that 'action research provides a means whereby research can become a systematic intervention going beyond describing, analysing, and theorizing social practice to working in partnership with participants to reconstruct and transform those practices' (2006: 27).

As a student teacher on placement (essentially a 'guest' in school), or a beginning teacher, you may feel you have little right or access to real agency. On the other hand, your school colleagues may have high expectations of you as someone they hope will have fresh ideas and help them to 're-energize' their teaching. You may have more influence than you think to affect changes or improvements through your research.

Research needs to demonstrate some *relevance* in terms of its purpose:

> Researchers need to show how their work relates to things that matter and it is in this sense that good research calls upon researchers to *demonstrate* the relevance of what they have done. The relevance should never be taken for granted; it should never be assumed to 'speak for itself'.
>
> (Denscombe 2002: 61)

The question of 'relevance' is a complex one for in many ways relevance is relative; what may be considered relevant for one person in one context may not be in others. Without wishing to be dismissive of this issue, space here does not permit in-depth exploration of the issue; suffice it to say, the scope and nature of relevance will be varied in different situations. Hammersley (1992: 74-6) discusses relevance in terms of thinking about the audience you might be researching for, its contribution to existing knowledge for fellow researchers, and how it might inform practice. Hammersley (2002) also gives a helpful account of Schutz's (1970) ideas of 'imposed relevance' to a 'problem', in terms of its Greek root 'that which is thrown before me' (in other words, an issue that you come across you feel needs to be explored) and 'intrinsic' relevance that, in simple terms, might be something that we as humans, being naturally curious about the world, want to look at more closely, for the sake of improving it.

You may become involved in research with colleagues, to make sense of and hopefully improve an issue that may affect many pupils. *Collaboration* can provide a powerful driver for necessary or desired change in a school. The nature and benefits of researching with others have been explored in Chapter 9. There is something powerful and motivating about being part of a process with others; this alone may be educative. As a student, beginning or experienced teacher, researching with colleagues will allow you to gain access to their insights of many aspects of the school and their work, which may be very different to yours and may shape your thinking.

The scope or ambition of what can be achieved can be increased with more researchers working in one area. On the other hand, researching with people you already work with as teaching colleagues can be tricky; many perspectives on methods or purposes of the research may be difficult to negotiate. In the research process, viewpoints shift and everyday concerns of teaching can get in the way; individuals may leave or school/ departmental priorities alter, either because of an externally imposed driver, or an internal change, for example leadership. Researching with your colleagues may be a mixed experience. The 'bottom line' for you may be to ensure you can undertake research to meet deadlines, for example as a student teacher for university assignments or meet the requirements for passing your induction year as a beginning teacher.

Working with colleagues as the *subjects* of your research (the 'researched') is quite a different matter with its own issues. Inevitably, you will not find universal support for, or acknowledgement of the value of your research, among all your colleagues; this is disheartening but as a student or beginning teacher you may not have the status within your school to change very entrenched views about the perceived worth of educational research (of any kind) in the minds of some of your colleagues. Even a well-established and experienced teacher may find a similar situation. Dadds (1995) gives an excellent account of an experienced teacher undertaking research in her school where her colleagues are her research subjects; there are many lessons to be taken from this teacher's 'story'; for example, not least, the account of how research has to be 'fitted in' in less than ideal ways and in the light of colleagues' more or less supportive views of her work.

An important challenge is how you manage that most precious of commodities – time. 'Good research should always be aware of how it connects with theories, practices and problems that already exist' (Denscombe 2002: 60); it is important to explore other people's views in order to challenge your existing ideas and gain a range of perspectives. Your reading may continue throughout a research project, and influence your thinking at different points. However, attempting to read and make sense of everything written and thought about in your area of interest is not achievable and is likely to lead to 'exploding head syndrome', a state of mind characterized by sleeplessness, confusion and inability to act! So, be realistic about what you can read in the time you have, acknowledging that there will always be literature you will miss, or other views you might have sought (see Chapter 4).

As already mentioned, with (lack of) time in mind, it will be essential to choose a narrow focus. You will have a defined space of time in which to complete your research activity; this will be helpful (nothing like a deadline to focus the mind) but also frustrating. You may begin by thinking your research will be easily achievable in the time you have but this may not be the case. If we believe that knowledge is provisional and also in research nothing ever really 'ends' just because you are looking at it and thinking about it, you may be left feeling there is so much more to know and do; you will be right. Much research ends because of externally imposed deadlines and these arbitrary points in time might not match the way your work progresses. You will need to live with this uncertainty, acknowledge it in your work and even embrace it 'without chaos, no knowledge' (Feyerabend 1993: 158). Sometimes there is a need to live with confusion and lack of clarity; most research presents more questions than answers. This is what makes it so rich and rewarding.

The issue of *power* in research (which you may be familiar with) is worth exploring. You may be using your pupils as your research subjects (who you have power over as their teacher) or your colleagues; some will be your senior in the school hierarchy. If you are a student teacher, a temporary 'guest' on placement, your position in relation to others is particularly interesting. The fact that your colleagues may be more or less supportive of your research has already been discussed. Because your colleagues and mentors assess your teaching whatever their views of your research, they have power over you as a student. However, as a researcher you *always* have power over your subjects; you decide how situations or people's views are represented in your research (Bloom 1998: 35). Dadds (1995) explores the issue of how the teacher researcher deals with 'uncomfortable' data, for example views expressed by teachers that may be considered inappropriate. Does she have a duty to reveal the views, or simply exclude them from her final account (see Chapter 5 concerning ethical issues)? This will be doubly difficult if you are a student or beginning teacher; will you be able to write material that shows the colleagues who assess you negatively? Teacher researchers are different from many other kinds of researcher; they have to continue to work with their colleagues when research finishes and must take account of this.

There is one final phenomenon that will present challenges for you now and in the future – *values*. Your values will inevitably impact upon and be present within your research, from the areas you choose to look at, the ways you work with others and how you represent the experience. Values are complex and there is much for you to consider in relation to your own and those of participants. For example 'research is not helped by making it appear value-free. It is better to give the reader a good look at the researcher' (Stake 1995: 95). Whatever stage you are at in your career, you will have ideas and views about education, informed by your own (more or less recent) experiences of schooling (and further/higher education) and life in general. If you are inexperienced as a teacher, your views may differ to those of your colleagues; this may or may not prove to be problematic in all your learning and development not just your research. It will be important to be aware of your position and views and acknowledge and challenge them wherever you can. Ask yourself often 'What's going on here? Why do I think that?'

To challenge your own position, you can encourage others' criticisms of your views. Altrichter (2005: 29) suggests that the use of a research diary, not only as a record of thoughts and ideas, but also to invite a process of challenging those ideas, helps us to be aware of our underlying assumptions and values that we bring to our research. In the writing up of our research, however hard we try, our values and viewpoints may always be present. Geertz (1988: 50) wrote about the 'voice' of ethnographers in their work: 'The way of saying is the what of saying'; even our choice of words to describe things reveals us in certain ways, however hard we might try to be 'neutral'.

The reasons for continuing study and research and the various means of achieving this

While it is possible to undertake research without being registered for study with a university or higher education institution, there are many advantages to completing research that is accredited; you are working towards gaining a highly regarded academic qualification that has recognized currency and is considered to be excellent professional development whatever direction your future career takes. As noted above, the Professional Standards for Teachers (DfES 2007) include specific references to engaging with professional development (for example teachers at the 'Core' stage will 'Evaluate their performance and be committed to improving their practice through appropriate professional development' (C7, DfES 2007)) and with research and enquiry (for example teachers at the 'Excellent' stage will 'Research and evaluate innovative curricular practices and draw on research outcomes and other sources of external evidence to inform their own practice and that of colleagues' (E2, DfES 2007).

A further advantage of undertaking research through a programme of study is learning with others; sharing ideas, successes and frustrations can be very sustaining. Your peers on a Masters of Art (MA) or Masters of Education (MEd) programme will support and challenge your views giving valuable alternative perspectives. You will have access to the knowledge and experience of tutors, who are most likely to have undertaken (and be undertaking) similar kinds of research in education or related fields; they can offer excellent support and guidance and are likely to have encountered any problems you come across. A university tutor once said to a group of new Masters' students 'prepare to be disrupted'; how right he was. Taught sessions may challenge your assumptions, drawing upon contemporary thinking in education and research. Many Masters degrees involve engaging with different research methods that may influence the areas of research you choose. You will also have access to excellent libraries, learning resources and affiliated services, to advise and support you, for example, with developing academic writing and how to present and publish your work.

If you are convinced that Masters level study is for you, there are several options. Many courses are part time, lasting two or three years and involve attendance at early evening, or weekend sessions. Online tutor support is usually available. Some programmes have a clear focus, for example, related to a particular subject, or areas such as leadership and management. Others are more generic, for example 'MA in Education'. This may allow you to study alongside colleagues who work in different sectors and roles, and can make for rich insights and experiences. There are also programmes offering study completely by distance learning; others have a mixture of face-to-face teaching and online learning. In making your choice, you need to consider what mode of study most suits you and whether a programme with a particular emphasis, or not, is what you are interested in. Think about your current situation and your future career plans in considering the options. It will also be worth looking at details; this may be what makes you choose one course above another. For example, how does the course design take account of teachers' busy lives? Are there flexible submission dates for assessed work? Are the assessed items varied?

Most teachers undertake their study (and, therefore, their research) part time, alongside their teaching; however there are full-time one-year programmes. Some teachers negotiate a secondment to take a Masters degree in a year, or they may take a term off work, especially if the research they are undertaking is related to a whole-school issue for a sustained period of study for part of the course. Having gained a Masters degree, you may have 'caught the bug' so much that you want to continue. The next step is to enrol for MPhil or PhD study; many universities offering MA programmes will have opportunities for you to carry on with your research. PhD study can be taken on a part- or full-time basis. You may gain funding for a full-time PhD from a university and teach students in higher education alongside your study. You may also work as part of a research team in a university, undertaking research projects that external bodies contract, which could be in education, or other public service settings, such as the NHS or Social Services, in a wide range of areas. Some very large, long-term research projects may be undertaken with colleagues from other universities, drawing on a broad range of data and processes over a period of time.

The concluding section includes two case studies of research under-taken in very different educational settings, presented as assignments of part-time students on an MA in Education course. Both teachers were experienced, but new to researching. They represent in a small way the diversity of work that is possible in researching your own practice or educational context. They show that if you want to look at something closely, think about it, locate it in the wider world of related thinking and say something about it, real improvements can be made to young people's education.

Case Study 1

> The Head of Department of Religious Education (RE) in a Church of England secondary school for one of her MA programme assignments considered how the use of thinking skills could improve the progress of an able group of pupils in Year 10. She considered cognitive development, moral development and faith development in relation to each other and what might be considered 'progress' in RE, relating these areas to thinking skills. She went on to evaluate different RE teaching resources, which claimed to include and promote thinking skills, enabling pupils to move from abstract to concrete ideas.

Reflection on Case Study 1

Many significant moral and ethical issues were explored, through thinking skills, which, through collaborative learning, allowed significant progress for pupils to engage with issues of relevance to them, making the point that the power of thinking skills is not intrinsic, but how, when linked to certain content, they can facilitate greater understanding of particular important subject issues. This was an intense examination of a highly specific issue within one person's practice, which was related to extensive wider reading, with a positive impact of the writer's practice and pupils' learning.

Case Study 2

> A teacher working at a residential college for young people with physical and learning disabilities reflected on the quality of dance produced by students working with a local dance group and theatre. This experience was considered in developing teaching of dance

within the college, with very positive outcomes. One of the worthwhile (and very unusual) additions to presenting written research was the production of a DVD that showed the students performing their dance pieces. The project underwent external evaluation also, and the assignment reflects upon this.

Reflection on Case Study 2

The account of the project challenged the reader in terms of the ways of conceiving limitations and capabilities of young people with complex needs; in this case, the young people operated on an equal footing with professional dancers and performers. This piece of work, considering an event happening over a few days, in one place, is an excellent example of how giving an account of it to others not only alters practice and thinking within an institution already successfully enabling a group of young people to achieve, but also affects every reader who comes into contact with it, creating significant shifts in thinking and attitudes.

Conclusion ... next steps

Having raised various issues for you as a beginning researcher, it is hoped that you have been able to gain a sense of the possible issues, as you embark upon research while teaching. You are in a complex position; learning about yourself, about teaching and learning and yet, this is also the content of your occupation, working with young people's learning every day. Your research may help you to understand and do this better, as it will give you access to additional layers of thinking and experience. You will find the journey exciting, frustrating, challenging and rich; if you enjoy learning (which you must, as you have chosen to teach) it is almost certain you will enjoy research, as it involves learning in large amounts. It is hoped that you will feel motivated to begin and continue your research however you decide to develop your career, for example as an expert in your subject, an inspiration to your colleagues and pupils, an advocate for action research or a dynamic leader.

Glossary

agency   the ability of an individual or group to influence situations and issues, to varying degrees, to instigate change.

collaboration working together with others in research; this can mean several people working as researchers on different/similar aspects of a research area/question, for example in data-gathering, analysis and formulating resulting theories/conclusions/actions.

multidimensional in research, related to the notion that in any context, there are likely to be many different perspectives at play; it may or may not be possible to take account of and represent the varying points of view, but it may be important to acknowledge their existence.

power an important ethical issue that is related to the relationship between the researcher and researched; this can be more complex than at first thought, especially when teachers research their work and working context, that is when the researcher already has a relationship with the subjects of their research (for example pupils, colleagues, parents, governors) and has to continue with this existing relationship following the research activity.

professionalism the notion that there is a set of shared values/ behaviours/knowledge and understanding associated with a particular group of people working in the same area which, in a research context, will influence the choice of area to be researched, how research is approached and resulting analysis/conclusions.

values the set of beliefs/attitudes/views that any individual brings to a research situation, which may be likely to affect/inform/influence any number of choices about research, for example the area to be researched, methodologies and methods, conclusions drawn and proposed actions arising from these.

References

Addison, N. and Burgess, L. (2000) *Learning to Teach Art and Design in the Secondary School*. London and New York: Routledge Falmer.

Altrichter, H. (2005) *Research Methods in the Social Sciences*. London: Sage Publications.

Altrichter, H., Posch, P. and Somekh, B. (1993) *Teachers Investigate Their Work*. London: Routledge.

Bloom, R. L. (1998) *Under the Sign of Hope: Feminist Methodology and Narrative Interpretation*. New York: State University of New York Press.

Carr, D. (2003) *Making Sense of Education: An Introduction to the Philosophy and Theory of Education and Teaching*. London: Routledge Falmer.

Dadds, M. (1995) *Passionate Enquiry and School Development: A Story About Teacher Action Research*. London and Bristol, PA: Falmer Press.

Denscombe, M. (2002) *Ground Rules for Good Research*. Buckingham: Open University Press.

DfES (Department for Education and Skills) (2007) *Professional Standards for Teachers*, www.tda.gov.uk/upload/resources/pdt/s/standards_qts.pdf, accessed 20 June 2007.

Elliot, J. (1991) *Action Research for Educational Change*. Buckingham, UK and Bristol, PA: Open University Press.

Feyerabend, P. (1993) *Against Method: Outline of an Anarchistic Theory of Knowledge*. London: Verso.

Geertz, C. (1988) *Works and Lives: The Anthropologist as Author*. Stanford, CA: Stanford University Press.

Hammersley, M. (1992) *What's Wrong with Ethnography?* London: Routledge.

Hammersley, M. (2002) Action research: a contradiction in terms? Paper presented at the Annual Conference of the British Educational Research Association, University of Exeter, England, 12–14 September, www.leeds.ac.uk/educol/documents/00002130.htm, accessed 16 September 2006.

Schutz, A. (1970) *Reflections on the Problem of Relevance*. New Haven: Yale University Press.

Somekh, B. (2006) *Action Research: A Methodology for Change and Development*. Maidenhead: Open University Press.

Somekh, B. and Lewin, C. (2005) *Research Methods in the Social Sciences*. London: Sage Publications.

Stake, R. (1995) *The Art of Case Study Research*. Thousand Oaks, CA: Sage Publications.

Key texts

Dadds, M. (1995) *Passionate Enquiry and School Development: A Story About Teacher Action Research*. London and Bristol, PA: Falmer Press. A very 'readable' account of a teacher's research 'journey' highlighting the practical concerns of researching with your colleagues, the problems of finding time for research and many other issues that will strike a chord if you are researching in a school.

House, E. R. and Howe, K. R. (1999) *Values in Evaluation and Social Research*. California: Sage Publications. This text presents a very thorough examination of the nature and position of values in research. Although the book seems primarily aimed at researchers who undertake evaluations of various contexts, many of the issues raised are relevant for any kind of research, in any context.

Somekh, B. (2006) *Action Research: A Methodology for Change and Development*. Maidenhead: Open University Press. Bridget Somekh has been involved with action research for many years and in this book explores it as a means of individuals examining change through research in order to make 'systematic interventions' in their work.

Somekh, B. and Lewin, C. (2005) *Research Methods in the Social Sciences*. London: Sage Publications. This text provides an account of many methodologies, methods and approaches in research. In each chapter different issues and theories are explored in some depth. 'Stories from the field' in each chapter elaborate 'key concepts' and there are many invaluable suggestions for further reading. This is an accessible, excellent reference book with contributions from experienced researchers in a broad range of fields, with varying positions on many important issues in research.

Index